ULTIMATE HOCKEY TRIVIA

Don Weekes

Kerry Banks

GREYSTONE BOOKS
Douglas & McIntyre
Vancouver/Toronto

For the van Vlaardingens: my wife Caroline, Aad and Kitty, Peter, Kathy, Laura and Adam.—Don Weekes

For Eddie: who bought me my first pair of blades.—Kerry Banks

Greystone Books
A division of Douglas & McIntyre
1615 Venables Street
Vancouver, British Columbia V5L 2H1

Canadian Cataloguing in Publication Data
Weekes, Don.
 Ultimate hockey trivia
 ISBN I-55054-507-8
 1. National Hockey League—Miscellanea. 2. Hockey—Miscellanea. I.
Banks, Kerry, 1952– II. Title
GV847.W426 1996 796.962 C96-910231-3

Editing by Anne Rose and Kerry Banks
Design by Peter Cocking
Typesetting by Vancouver Desktop Publishing
Cover photo by Bruce Bennett/Bruce Bennett Studios
Printed and bound in Canada by Best Book Manufacturers
Printed on acid-free paper ∞

The publisher gratefully acknowledges the assistance of the Canadian Council and of the British Columbia Ministry of Tourism, Small Business and Culture.

Don Weekes *is a television producer and writer with* CFCF *12 in Montreal. He recently completed the documentary* Passing the Torch, *the story of the building of Molson Centre. This is his eighth hockey trivia quiz book.*

Kerry Banks *is an award-winning magazine features writer, a sports columnist and* TV *sports commentator. He lives in Vancouver.*

CONTENTS

PREFACE

Some hockey seasons are more special than others. Who knows why? Maybe it's some cosmic alignment of the planets that produces a year in which a pack of players suddenly strike stardom and a host of long-standing NHL records are erased from the books. Or maybe it's simply a case of several good teams graduating to greatness at the same time, making their mark with the right coach and system.

Perhaps it was the hockey gods, who, after 1994–95's bitter lockout, deemed that the faithful deserved a blockbuster comeback season. After all, when was the last time Mario Lemieux was healthy enough to play 70 games; the last time four players joined the 500-goal club in the same year; the last time a netminder scored a goal; or the last time a relocated franchise, in its first season, won a Stanley Cup?

How about "the Trade"—St. Patrick of Montreal helping Denver win its first professional sports championship; the wacky rat craze in Florida; Detroit's five-man Russian unit; Paul Coffey becoming the league's first 1,000-assist defenseman; and the rise of Scotty Bowman to the top of the most-games-coached list?

And, too, we can't forget the lows of 1995–96: the botched trade of Wayne Gretzky; Pavel Bure's season-ending knee injury; the loss of yet another Canadian franchise; the Ottawa Senators' fourth consecutive last-place finish; and the defending champion New Jersey Devils' fall from grace.

Like all the trivia books of this series, this edition recounts the best stories of a century of hockey, but with special attention to 1995–96, a season that gave us Mario Lemieux, Joe Sakic and Paul Kariya, but also the video voodoo of the Fox network's $3-million glowing puck.

DON WEEKES, KERRY BANKS
July 1, 1996

1

BUSTING OUT OF THE BLOCKS

Each hockey season brings new hope and challenges for players and teams alike. For NHL rookies, their first season and first game are always memorable, if only to them. But one rookie will long be known for how he busted out of the blocks: Toronto's Gus Bodnar scored the fastest goal by a rookie in his first NHL game. Bodnar scored just 15 seconds after stepping onto the ice on October 30, 1943. In this warm-up chapter, we set our sights mostly on recent records and highlights to get you trivia rookies off to a fast start.

(Answers are on page 5)

1.1 Jaromir Jagr scored 149 points in 1995–96, breaking whose record for most points in a season by a European-born player?
A. Jari Kurri's
B. Teemu Selanne's
C. Kent Nilsson's
D. Peter Stastny's

1.2 Who is nicknamed "Mighty Mouse"?
A. Theoren Fleury
B. Paul Kariya
C. Doug Gilmour
D. Cliff Ronning

1.3 Who scored his 500th NHL goal at Nassau Coliseum in 1995-96, only to have the feat ignored by the public address announcer?
A. Mark Messier
B. Dale Hawerchuk
C. Steve Yzerman
D. Mario Lemieux

1.4 How much money did the Winnipeg Jets pay Keith Tkachuk in order to match the five-year deal he was offered by the Chicago Blackhawks in 1995?
A. $10.2 million
B. $13.2 million
C. $17.2 million
D. $20.2 million

1.5 When asked who he thought was the NHL's dirtiest player, who responded: "Can I vote for myself?"
A. Ulf Samuelsson
B. Mike Peluso
C. Chris Chelios
D. Bryan Marchment

1.6 Who said, "Around here, the C stands for 'see ya later!'"?
A. Randy Cunneyworth
B. Wendel Clark
C. Mike Keane
D. Brett Hull

1.7 Which goalkeeper owns the NHL record for most career losses?
A. Gump Worsley
B. Terry Sawchuk
C. Gilles Meloche
D. Harry Lumley

1.8 What sport did Colorado Avalanche defenseman Uwe Krupp participate in while recovering from a knee injury in 1995–96?
A. Fencing
B. Dogsledding
C. Curling
D. Ice yachting

1.9 When the Montreal Forum closed its doors on March 11, 1996, the Canadiens held a charity auction that saw everything from rink scrapers to hot-dog grills go on the block. Which item attracted the highest bid?
A. Captain Pierre Turgeon's locker
B. The Canadiens' 1993 Stanley Cup banner
C. The Canadiens' dressing-room door
D. Ex-NHL president Clarence Campbell's seat

1.10 Which Hockey Hall-of-Famer competed for Canada in the pole vault at the 1936 Berlin Olympics?
A. Syl Apps
B. Lynn Patrick
C. Neil Colville
D. Lionel Conacher

1.11 In which NHL arena did Jean-Claude Van Damme battle terrorists in the 1995 movie *Sudden Death?*
A. Pittsburgh's Civic Arena
B. Tampa Bay's ThunderDome
C. Los Angeles' Great Western Forum
D. New York's Madison Square Garden

1.12 Who scored the highest percentage of his team's goals in 1995–96?
A. The Mighty Ducks of Anaheim's Paul Kariya
B. The Pittsburgh Penguins' Mario Lemieux
C. The Washington Capitals' Peter Bondra
D. The Vancouver Canucks' Alexander Mogilny

1.13 Which team's mascot had to be rescued after he fell into a pit of fire during pre-game ceremonies at the club's 1995–96 home opener?
A. The New Jersey Devils'
B. The Calgary Flames'
C. The Florida Panthers'
D. The Mighty Ducks of Anaheim's

1.14 How many stitches was Hall-of-Famer Eddie Shore estimated to have acquired during his NHL career?
A. 600
B. 700
C. 800
D. 900

1.15 How did Canadian import player Tony Job make headlines in the Italian Hockey League in 1995–96?
A. He scored eight goals in one game
B. He married an Italian movie star
C. He tried to set fire to an opponent's sweater
D. He sang on stage with Luciano Pavarotti

1.16 Which NHLer's father won three medals in swimming at the 1972 Olympic Games?
A. Pavel Bure's
B. Neal Broten's
C. Mikael Renberg's
D. Jaromir Jagr's

1.17 What was Tie Domi's punishment for decking Ulf Samuelsson with a sucker punch in 1995–96?
A. A five-game suspension and a $500 fine
B. An eight-game suspension and a $1,000 fine
C. A 10-game suspension and a $5,000 fine
D. A 15-game suspension and a $2,000 fine

1.18 Whose jersey number did the Montreal Canadiens retire on October 7, 1995?

A. Jacques Plante's
B. Guy Lafleur's
C. Henri Richard's
D. Bernie Geoffrion's

1.19 In 1995, the world's largest hockey stick was erected outside the United States Hockey Hall of Fame. In which state will you find it?

A. Michigan
B. Illinois
C. Minnesota
D. Pennsylvania

BUSTING OUT OF THE BLOCKS
Answers

1.1 D. Peter Stastny's
The native of Bratislava, Czechoslovakia, burst onto the NHL scene in 1980–81, recording 109 points for the Quebec Nordiques and capturing the rookie-of-the-year award. It was the first of six consecutive 100-point seasons for Stastny, who enjoyed his best offensive campaign in 1981–82. Playing on a line with brothers, Anton and Marian, he tallied 139 points (46 G, 93 A) to finish third in the scoring race behind Wayne Gretzky and Mike Bossy. No other European player would surpass Stastny's output until 1995–96, when Jaromir Jagr hit the 149-point mark.

1.2 B. Paul Kariya
Former linemate Todd Krygier hung the tag "Mickey

Mouse" on Kariya, a fitting moniker for someone who plays in a city whose most famous citizens are cartoon characters. A lack of size was one of the few question marks about Kariya when he entered the NHL as a five-foot-10, 157-pound rookie in 1994–95. After spending the summer pumping iron, the little winger added 20 pounds of muscle to complement his dazzling skating and playmaking skills. There was certainly nothing Mickey Mouse about the results, as Kariya placed seventh in NHL scoring in 1995–96, with 108 points on 50 goals and 58 assists.

1.3 D. Mario Lemieux
The scorekeeper was clearly asleep at the switch when No. 66 notched his 500th career goal against the New York Islanders on October 26, 1995. The milestone marker, which capped a three-goal performance by Lemieux in a 7–5 Pens victory, was never revealed to the sparse crowd of 8,384 at Nassau Coliseum. "I was waiting for it. I was surprised they didn't announce it," said Lemieux, who reached the 500-goal plateau faster than anyone in NHL history except Wayne Gretzky.

The NHL's Fastest 500-Goal Scorers			
Player	**Date**	**Game No.**	**Goaltender**
Wayne Gretzky	Nov. 22/86	575	Empty net
Mario Lemieux	Oct. 26/95	605	Tommy Soderstrom
Mike Bossy	Jan. 2/86	647	Empty net
Phil Esposito	Dec. 22/74	803	Jim Rutherford
Jari Kurri	Oct. 17/92	833	Empty net
Bobby Hull	Feb. 17/70	861	Ed Giacomin

1.4 C. $17.2 million
Tkachuk vaulted into the penthouse of NHL wage earners when he signed a five-year, $17.2-million contract with the Winnipeg Jets in October 1995. An unrestricted

free agent at the start of the 1995–96 season, Tkachuk was free to entertain offers from other teams when he and the Jets failed to ink a new deal. Chicago tried to steal him away by offering an enormous sum (a front-loaded contract worth $6 million in the first year alone), but the cash-strapped Jets bit the bullet and matched the offer.

1.5 A. Ulf Samuelsson

In a 1995 issue of *Sports Illustrated*, 56 anonymous NHL veterans were asked to select the dirtiest player in the league. Samuelsson collected 26 votes. Bryan Marchment was a distant second with nine. As is evident by his quote, Samuelsson doesn't mind the label. Universally loathed by opposition players and fans alike, the Swedish D-man is known as a cheap-shot artist. It was a Samuelsson knee that put Boston forward Cam Neely out of action for a year in 1991 and later ended his career. Yet, despite his villainous reputation, as of 1996 Samuelsson had only been suspended once by the NHL. He missed three non- game days and was fined $8,697 for engaging in a stick-swinging duel with Mark Messier on March 5, 1993.

1.6 C. Mike Keane

Prophetically, Keane made this quip when he was named captain of the Montreal Canadiens in April 1995. Keane, of course, was traded to Colorado in the Patrick Roy deal in December 1995. Keane was the fourth consecutive Canadiens captain to be traded in a six-year period. The others sent packing were Chris Chelios, Guy Carbonneau and Kirk Muller. Once considered a badge of honour and a sign of stability, the Montreal C has come to represent something else entirely—a bull's-eye.

1.7 A. Gump Worsley

Worsley won 335 games and lost 353, which makes

him the lone netminder among the NHL's top 15 career-victory leaders with a winning percentage below .500. The stat is more a reflection of where Worsley played than of his ability, though. For the first decade of his career, he tended goal for the hapless New York Rangers. Playing behind the Blueshirts' porous defense, Worsley faced a steady barrage of rubber. A reporter once asked Gump which team gave him the most trouble. The pint-sized New York goalie answered without hesitation, "The Rangers." Worsley's fortunes got a boost in 1963 when he was traded to Montreal, where he later won two Vezina Trophies as the NHL's top netminder and four Stanley Cups.

Most Career Losses by NHL Goalies					
Losses	Player	GP	Decisions	Wins	Ties
353	Gump Worsley	862	839	335	151
351	Gilles Meloche	788	752	270	131
330	Terry Sawchuk	971	950	447	173
327	Glenn Hall	906	897	407	165
326	Harry Lumley	804	802	333	143

1.8   B. Dogsledding
During his rehab from a knee injury, Uwe Krupp was given permission by Colorado's team doctors to pursue his other sporting passion—dogsled racing. The German-born Krupp owns a team of Siberian huskies and has entered several races in Colorado. Ultimately, when his hockey playing days are finished, he would like to move to Alaska and compete in the gruelling 1,159-mile Iditarod Trail Dog Sled Race from Anchorage to Nome.

1.9   B. The Canadiens' 1993 Stanley Cup banner
Pierre Daoust, the owner of a suburban Montreal bar, spent $32,000, plus $4,000 in taxes, for the Canadiens' most recent Stanley Cup banner. It was the highest

price paid for any of the 145 items up for auction. The charity fund-raiser drew 2,500 people, who spent $726,750 on a wide array of memorabilia, including shot clocks, stick racks, autographed sweaters and even a latrine from the Forum washroom. One item that didn't go on the block was an original seat from section 111. An ingenious thief, equipped with a pair of bolt cutters, had spirited it out of the Forum during a game a month earlier against the Ottawa Senators.

1.10 A. Syl Apps
Apps was a superb all-round athlete, who starred in football, hockey and track and field at Hamilton's McMaster University. His speciality was the pole vault, and in 1934 he won the British Empire Games pole-vaulting championship in London, England. In 1936, he represented Canada in the pole vault at the Berlin Olympics, placing sixth. Apps joined the Toronto Maple Leafs shortly afterwards and went on to lead the club in scoring and win the Calder Trophy as the NHL's top rookie. The smooth-skating centre was Toronto's inspirational leader and captain during the team's golden era of the late 1940s.

1.11 A. Pittsburgh's Civic Arena
Many of the scenes in the film *Sudden Death*, in which Jean-Claude Van Damme plays a fire chief fighting a deadly duel with terrorists during game seven of the Stanley Cup finals, were shot during an actual game between the Penguins and the Blackhawks at Pittsburgh's Civic Arena. The Igloo was chosen as the backdrop for the action thriller because Penguins owner Howard Baldwin was one of the film's producers. In fact, the movie was based on an idea proposed by Baldwin's wife, Karen.

1.12 C. The Washington Capitals' Peter Bondra
No NHL team relies on one scorer as much as the Capitals

depend on Peter Bondra. He accounted for 22 per cent of his club's goal scoring in 1995–96, the highest mark in the league. The figure is doubly impressive as Bondra missed 15 games due to injuries and a contract dispute. Counting only the games he played in, he actually scored 27 per cent of his team's goals. Bondra also led the NHL in the category in 1994–95, when he scored 25 per cent of the Caps' goals.

1995-96's Percentage of Team Goals

Player	Team	Team Goals	Player Goals	Pct.
Peter Bondra	Capitals	234	52	22.2
Paul Kariya	Ducks	234	50	21.4
Alex Mogilny	Canucks	278	55	19.8
Brett Hull	Blues	219	43	19.6
Theo Fleury	Flames	241	46	19.1
Mario Lemieux	Penguins	362	69	19.1

1.13 D. The Mighty Ducks of Anaheim's

White Wing, Anaheim's web-footed mascot, was nearly barbecued prior to the team's 1995–96 home opener when he tried to bounce off a mini-trampoline to sail through fire, only to stumble and fall into a gas-powered wall of flames. The impromptu roasting was just one of the misfortunes that befell the Ducks' bumbling mascot in 1995–96. On another occasion, White Wing was left dangling helplessly in midair when the rigging that lowers him to the ice during the pre-game show jammed.

1.14 D. 900

No one ever played hockey with more reckless abandon than Eddie Shore. During his 14-year NHL career, the hardrock Boston D-man antagonized fans, fought opponents, harassed officials and ignited countless controversies. A perpetual target of rival players, who would often gang up in twos and threes to nail him, Shore paid a heavy toll in injuries. His face and body were embroidered with more than 900 stitches and he suffered fractures to his hip, back and collarbone. His nose was broken 14 times, his jaw smashed five times and he had almost every tooth in his mouth knocked out. But nothing ever stopped Shore for long. Still brawling and banging at age 37, he led Boston to the Stanley Cup in 1939.

1.15 C. He tried to set fire to an opponent's sweater
With Italian spectators screaming abuse, TV cameras caught Canadian Tony Job trying to set an opposition player's sweater on fire with a lighter taken from the debris thrown on the ice during a bench-clearing brawl. The bizarre incident occurred during game two of the best-of-seven Italian League final series between Milan and Bolzano in April 1996. Fortunately, the jersey didn't ignite.

1.16 A. Pavel Bure's
Vladimir Bure, a world-class swimmer, was awarded the Order of Lenin for his athletic achievements. He won three medals at the 1972 Munich Olympics: a bronze in the 100-metre freestyle, a silver in the 4 x 100-metre freestyle relay and a bronze in the 4 x 200-metre freestyle relay.

1.17 B. An eight-game suspension and a $1,000 fine
It is hard to say who got the worst of a run-in between Tie Domi and Ulf Samuelsson in a game at Toronto's Maple Leaf Gardens on October 14, 1995. The two players initially bumped behind the Rangers' net and continued to jostle as they made their way to the front of the crease. Domi then dropped his left glove and delivered a blow with his fist, striking the unsuspecting Samuelsson squarely on the chin. The Swede fell backwards and struck his head on the ice. He needed four

stitches to close the gash and suffered a concussion. As punishment for his sneak attack, Domi received an eight-game suspension and a $1,000 fine.

1.18 A. Jacques Plante's
More than 40 goalies, including several Hall-of-Famers, have worn No. 1 in the long and glorious history of the Montreal Canadiens, but it was not until Montreal's 1995–96 home opener that the number was finally retired. Receiving the honour was the late Jacques Plante, the man who pioneered the use of the goalie mask. Jake the Snake wore No. 1 with the Habs from 1952 to 1963, a time span in which the Hall-of-Famer won the MVP award once and the Vezina Trophy as the NHL's top goalie six times.

1.19 C. Minnesota
The 107-foot hockey stick towers over the United States Hockey Hall of Fame in Eveleth, Minnesota. The Bunyanesque monument was built by the Christian Brothers hockey stick manufacturers from solid white and yellow Minnesota aspen. The blade has a woven fibreglass "slap sock" and the stick is painted and lacquered like all the company's playing-sized products. However, it is debatable whether it is actually the biggest hockey stick in the world. The town of Duncan, British Columbia, claims that the 207-foot stick that hangs outside its community centre merits the honour. Duncan's big stick was built by the Canadian government for the 1986 World's Fair in Vancouver. It too is made of solid wood and has hockey tape around the handle and blade. The Americans insist their stick is the genuine article because it was hauled to the site in one piece, while the Canadian giant had to be divided up so that it could be shipped. The residents of Duncan think that's just nitpicking.

GAME 1

MOST VALUABLE PLAYERS

Listed below are the first names of 25 Hart Trophy winners, those talented NHLers who earn MVP status each season. Once you figure out their last names, find them in the puzzle by reading across, down or diagonally. As with our 25th example, Andy B-A-T-H-G-A-T-E, connect the names by using letters no more than once. Start with the letters printed in heavy type.

(Solutions are on page 113)

Brett _____	Mark _____	Sid _____	Chuck _____
Bobby _____	Buddy _____	Stan _____	Guy _____
Bryan _____	Mario _____	Bernie _____	Jean _____
Ted _____	Elmer _____	Bobby _____	Gordie _____
Eric _____	Al _____	Wayne _____	Sergei _____
Maurice _____	Phil _____	Milt _____	Jacques _____
Andy _____			

```
E U C O R   Z T E R H
M L R L T R T K H O W G U
E F E T A K E Y R E L L X
A S I S O R O I F M I E U
L E S P B E R N E F A L P
R M B I O L I L O E G N T
  I A H E S F V E A U E
I K T G I R R E L L O Y D
T C S T A-T A D I N S R E
A H O R E A O Y N E R R N
I M O L C R L O R D R I N
D N E B A H O S D N A C E
  T N O C O   V I L H K
```

2

THE GUNS OF WINTER

When Steve Yzerman was "Stevie Wonder," the Detroit centre notched five 50-goal seasons, including 65- and 62-goal campaigns in 1988–89 and 1989–90. But Yzerman's style of play changed when defensive-mastermind Scotty Bowman came to the Red Wings. Yzerman became a complete two-way player, dropping his seasonal goal output and focussing on positional play. Keeping the goals-against averages down has become key not only to Detroit, but to Stanley Cup champions such as the 1995 New Jersey Devils and the 1996 Cup finalist Florida Panthers. In this chapter, we celebrate the Lemieuxs, Gretzkys and Hulls; and a few goal-scoring highlights worthy of the great "Stevie Wonder."

(Answers are on page 18)

2.1 **On February 23, 1996, Mario Lemieux and Jaromir Jagr became the second pair of teammates in NHL history to net their 50th goals in the same game. Which duo was the first to accomplish the feat?**
A. Montreal's Guy Lafleur and Steve Shutt
B. Pittsburgh's Mario Lemieux and Kevin Stevens
C. Calgary's Joe Mullen and Joe Nieuwendyk
D. Los Angeles' Jimmy Carson and Luc Robitaille

2.2 **Who is the lone member of the NHL's 500-goal club with fewer than 1,000 career points?**
A. Bobby Hull
B. Mike Bossy
C. Rocket Richard
D. Lanny McDonald

2.3 Which Florida Panther player's regular-season scoring exploits started the rubber-rat-throwing ritual that evolved into a full-scale mania during the 1996 playoffs?
A. Stu Barnes
B. Mike Hough
C. Scott Mellanby
D. Rob Niedermayer

2.4 Which NHL rookie made an immediate impact in 1995–96, scoring four goals with his first four shots on net?
A. The Sharks' Jan Caloun
B. The Oilers' Miroslav Satan
C. The Canadiens' Brian Savage
D. The Islanders' Todd Bertuzzi

2.5 Who was the oldest NHLer to win a scoring title?
A. Bill Cook
B. Elmer Lach
C. Gordie Howe
D. Phil Esposito

2.6 Which rookie scored two goals in four seconds in 1995–96 to tie the record for the fastest pair of goals in NHL annals?
A. The Hawks' Eric Daze
B. The Jets' Deron Quint
C. The Panthers' Radek Dvorak
D. The Senators' Daniel Alfredsson

2.7 Who is the only player to lead the NHL in goal scoring six seasons in a row?
A. Rocket Richard
B. Bobby Hull
C. Wayne Gretzky
D. Phil Esposito

2.8 How old was Gordie Howe when he posted his first 100-point NHL season?

A. 20
B. 30
C. 40
D. 50

2.9 In 1982–83, Wayne Gretzky scored 100 points faster than any other NHLer. How quickly did he reach the century mark?

A. In 34 games
B. In 44 games
C. In 54 games
D. In 64 games

2.10 Wayne Gretzky topped the Edmonton Oilers in goal scoring six times in eight years. How often did Gretzky lead the Los Angeles Kings in goal scoring during his seven seasons in Tinseltown?

A. Never
B. Once
C. Three times
D. Four times

2.11 Who holds the modern-day NHL record for goals scored in the most consecutive games?

A. Tim Kerr
B. Cam Neely
C. Charlie Simmer
D. Jari Kurri

2.12 Which of these snipers does *not* have a brother who has also played in the NHL?

A. Marcel Dionne
B. Mario Lemieux
C. Wayne Gretzky
D. Brett Hull

2.13 Only a select few NHLers have ever had a season in which they either scored or assisted on half of their team's total goals. Who posted the highest single-season percentage of his team's total offense?
A. Wayne Gretzky
B. Mario Lemieux
C. Marcel Dionne
D. Steve Yzerman

2.14 In order to renegotiate his contract with the Ottawa Senators in 1995–96, Alexei Yashin had to maintain a level of point production equal to the previous year. By how much did he fall short?
A. One point
B. Five points
C. 10 points
D. 20 points

2.15 How long did it take Alexander Mogilny to score his first NHL goal?
A. 20 seconds
B. Two minutes
C. Two periods
D. Two games

2.16 Since the advent of the 70-game schedule in 1949–50, one NHLer set the record for collecting both the most and the fewest penalty minutes in a season by a scoring champion. Who is he?
A. Gordie Howe
B. Mario Lemieux
C. Stan Mikita
D. Jean Béliveau

THE GUNS OF WINTER
Answers

2.1 B. Pittsburgh's Mario Lemieux and Kevin Stevens
The two Penguins both nailed goal number 50 against the Edmonton Oilers in a neutral site game in Cleveland, on March 21, 1993. Lemieux and Jaromir Jagr repeated the feat when they scored their 49th and 50th goals of 1995–96 against the Hartford Whalers. After they had both notched number 49, Lemieux bet Jagr a bottle of champagne to see who would be first to reach 50. Lemieux won the bubbly by a margin of three minutes 46 seconds.

2.2 C. Rocket Richard
The purest of goal scorers, Richard finished his career with 544 goals and 421 assists for 965 points. This is a remarkable ratio: 123 more goals than his assist total. Only one other player among the NHL's top 100 career-point leaders has posted 100 more goals than assists. (As of 1996, Brett Hull had 485 goals and 348 assists.) In the playoffs, Richard was even more of a goal-scoring specialist, recording nearly twice as many goals as assists: 82 to 44.

2.3 C. Scott Mellanby
On October 8, 1995, as the Florida Panthers prepared to take to the ice for their home opener, a rat appeared in the dressing room, causing a sudden ruckus. Displaying perfect shooting form, winger Scott Mellanby jumped up and dispatched the intruder to rat heaven with one swing of his hockey stick. "I one-timed it," joked Mellanby. The story might have died right there with the rodent, except that Mellanby went out and netted two goals that night as Florida beat the Calgary Flames 4–3. Panthers goalie John Vanbiesbrouck told reporters after the game that Mellanby didn't have a

hat trick, but he did have a "rat trick." The story was printed, Mellanby kept scoring, and a rain of rubber vermin soon began descending from the stands at the Miami Arena on a regular basis. During the playoffs, the ritual took a new turn as frenzied fans began tossing rats on the ice when any Panther scored.

2.4   A. The Sharks' Jan Caloun
San Jose's 1992 fourth-round pick was not supposed to be one of the Sharks' premier prospects, but Caloun's startling NHL debut may have caused the team to reassess its opinion. After being called up from the Kansas City Blades of the IHL on March 18, 1996, the Czech scored in his first game against Boston, then added two more in his second game versus Winnipeg and a fourth against Calgary in game three; all in only four shots on net. Caloun ended the season with eight goals on 20 shots, an accuracy rate of 40 per cent.

2.5   A. Bill Cook
In 1932–33, the New York Ranger captain won the NHL scoring title with 50 points in 48 games. Cook was 36 years five months old at the time, which makes him the oldest scoring champ in NHL annals. Gordie Howe, who ranks second on the greybeards' list, won his last scoring title at age 34, in 1962–63.

The NHL's Oldest Scoring Champs					
Player	**Age**	**Year**	**G**	**A**	**P**
Bill Cook	36.5	1932-33	28	22	50
Gordie Howe	34.11	1962-63	38	48	86
Newsy Lalonde	33.5	1920-21	33	8	41
Wayne Gretzky	33.2	1993-94	38	92	130
Roy Conacher	32.5	1948-49	26	42	68
Phil Esposito	32.1	1973-74	68	77	145

2.6 B. The Jets' Deron Quint

Quint scored only five goals in 1995–96, but the rookie defenseman put two of them behind Joaquin Gage of the Edmonton Oilers on December 15, 1995, in an amazing four seconds, equalling a Nels Stewart record that had stood since 1931. The goals came at 7:51 and 7:55 of the second period of a 9–4 Winnipeg win.

2.7 D. Phil Esposito

The Chicago Blackhawks never appreciated what a talent they had in Esposito. During his four years in the Windy City, the big, lumbering centre was dismissed as a "garbage collector," because he supposedly picked up points collecting Bobby Hull's leftovers. But after his trade to Boston in 1967–68, Espo confounded his critics by developing into the game's most deadly triggerman. For six straight seasons (1969–70 to 1974–75) he reigned supreme as the NHL's top goal scorer.

Espo's Six-Year Reign as the NHL's Top Gun				
Year	**Leader**	**Goals**	**Runner-Up**	**Goals**
1969-70	P. Esposito	43	S. Mikita	39
1970-71	P. Esposito	76	J. Bucyk	51
1971-72	P. Esposito	66	B. Hull/V. Hadfield	50
1972-73	P. Esposito	55	M. Redmond	52
1973-74	P. Esposito	68	R. Martin	52
1974-75	P. Esposito	61	G. Lafleur	53

2.8 C. 40

Howe was one day short of his 41st birthday when he registered his only 100-point NHL season, in 1968–69. He reached the century mark in the final game of the season, his 23rd NHL campaign. Despite his advanced age, Howe placed third in the scoring race with 103 points (44 G, 59 A), behind Phil Esposito and Bobby

Hull. The closest Howe had come to the 100-mark previously was in 1952–53, when he collected 95 points.

2.9 A. In 34 games
It is hard to imagine anyone breaking this record. Gretzky began the 1983–84 season as if he had been shot out of a cannon, counting point number 100 against the Winnipeg Jets on December 18, 1983, in only his 34th game of the season. Despite missing six games due to injury, Gretzky went on to amass 205 points and finish a whopping 79 points ahead of teammate Paul Coffey, the NHL's next highest scorer.

2.10 A. Never
Although Gretzky enjoyed several productive seasons in Los Angeles, his goal-scoring skills were on the wane by the time he joined the Kings in 1988. Bernie Nicholls led the Kings in goal scoring in Gretzky's first year in L.A., Luc Robitaille was top dog for the next five years, and Rick Tocchet was the Kings' leading sniper in the lockout-shortened 1994–1995 season.

2.11 C. Charlie Simmer
In 1979–80, Simmer scored goals in 13 straight games for the Los Angeles Kings, the longest string of any modern-day player. The output left him three games shy of equalling the all-time NHL mark of 16, set by Harry Broadbent of the Ottawa Senators in 1921–22.

2.12 D. Brett Hull
None of Hull's three brothers—Bobby, Jr., Blake and Bart—ever made the NHL. Mario Lemieux's older brother, Alain, played 119 games for St. Louis, Quebec and Pittsburgh in the 1980s; Wayne Gretzky's younger brother, Brent, played 13 games for Tampa Bay in 1993–94 and 1994–95; and Marcel Dionne's kid brother, Gilbert, played several years in the 1990s with Montreal, Philadelphia and Florida.

2.13 B. Mario Lemieux

Is Mario Lemieux the greatest offensive player of all time? This stat presents a strong argument for the case. Only four NHLers have ever had a season in which they figured in half of their team's total goals. Joe Malone and Cy Denneny accomplished the feat in the NHL's early days, when players often remained on the ice the entire game. Mario Lemieux and Wayne Gretzky are the only modern-day players to duplicate the deed. Lemieux's 1988–89 performance is in a class by itself. He either scored or assisted on an amazing 57.3 per cent of the goals scored by the Pittsburgh Penguins that season, the highest percentage in NHL history. Incredibly, Lemieux did not win the MVP award in 1988–89. It went to Gretzky, who recorded the same number of assists as Lemieux, but 31 fewer goals.

The NHL's One Player as Half a Team's Offense List*

Player	Year	Team Goals	G	A	PTS	Pct.
Mario Lemieux	1988-89	347	85	114	199	57.3
Joe Malone	1919-20	91	39	9	48	52.7
Mario Lemieux	1987-88	319	70	98	168	52.7
Wayne Gretzky	1984-85	401	73	135	208	51.9
Wayne Gretzky	1981-82	417	92	120	212	50.8
Cy Denneny	1924-25	83	27	15	42	50.6
Wayne Gretzky	1985-86	426	52	163	215	50.5
Wayne Gretzky	1980-81	328	55	109	164	50.0

Current to 1996.

2.14 A. One point

Alexei Yashin's 36-game holdout in 1995–96 was sparked by a dispute over a single point. Ottawa was prepared to renegotiate Yashin's contract if he equalled his scoring rate of the previous year. In 1993–94, Yashin tallied 79 points in 83 games, which works out to .952 points per game. In the lockout-shortened 1995 campaign, he compiled 44 points in 47 games, an average of .936 points per game—just .016 short of the target: .952. Had Yashin scored just one more point in 1995 (45 points in 47 games), his higher average of .957 would have contractually avoided the pettiness perpetrated by former Ottawa general manager Randy Sexton.

2.15 A. 20 seconds

Mogilny was the focus of attention for the 14,465 fans who jammed into Buffalo's Memorial Auditorium for the Sabres' home opener against the Quebec Nordiques on October 5, 1989. The talented Russian defector was billed as a "can't miss" prospect and the atmosphere inside the Aud was electric. Mogilny didn't disappoint. He began his NHL career with a bang, scoring on his first shot, 20 seconds into his first shift. The game, which Buffalo won 4–3, was clearly a special one for Mogilny, who brought one of his friends along to videotape the evening's events, right up to and including his first post-game shower.

2.16 C. Stan Mikita

In four of Mikita's first full six seasons in the NHL, he logged more than 100 minutes in penalties and earned a reputation as a tough and chippy player. In 1964–65, he won the scoring title while accumulating 154 PIM, the highest total by a scoring champion in NHL history. Two years later, he again won the Art Ross Trophy, but this time with just 12 PIM, the lowest total by a scoring champion since 1948–49. Mikita jokingly claims he made his remarkable midcareer conversion to Mr. Clean from Mr. Nasty after his daughter asked him why he was always sitting alone on the bench. It is more likely that he finally realized he was more useful to the Hawks on the ice than cooling his heels in the sin bin.

Scoring Champions with Most Penalty Minutes*

Player	Year	Team	GP	PTS	PIM
Stan Mikita	1964–65	Chi	70	87	154
Stan Mikita	1963–64	Chi	70	89	146
Jean Béliveau	1955–56	Mtl	70	88	143
Ted Lindsay	1949–50	Det	69	78	141
Bobby Orr	1969–70	Bos	76	120	125

Current to 1996.

Scoring Champions with Fewest Penalty Minutes*

Player	Year	Team	GP	PTS	PIM
Stan Mikita	1966-67	Chi	70	97	12
Stan Mikita	1967-68	Chi	72	87	14
Wayne Gretzky	1990-91	LA	78	163	16
Wayne Gretzky	1993-94	LA	81	130	20
Guy Lafleur	1976-77	Mtl	80	136	20

* Current to 1996/Minimum 70-game schedule.*

GAME 2

AUCTIONING OFF HISTORY

Just days before moving into their new home, the Molson Centre, the Montreal Canadiens held a charity auction at the old Montreal Forum to sell off everything from Stanley Cup banners to turnstiles. The March 1996 event raised more than $700,000. How much did each of the following Forum items finally sell for?

(Solutions are on page 113)

$500	$900	$900	$1,800
$2,250	$2,800	$3,400	$4,000
$4,750	$6,000	$7,500	$9,750
$11,500	$12,000	$15,000	$18,500
	$20,000	$32,000	

1. _____ Door to the Canadiens' dressing room.
2. _____ Forum hot-dog grill.
3. _____ Puck that scored the final Forum goal.
4. _____ Stanley Cup banner 1929–30.
5. _____ Forum countdown clock.
6. _____ Announcer Claude Mouton's microphone.
7. _____ "Forever Proud" banner.
8. _____ The Canadiens' bench.
9. _____ Forum turnstile.
10. _____ Goal net.
11. _____ Forum goal lights and post.
12. _____ Vincent Damphousse's locker.
13. _____ Forum ice scraper.
14. _____ Molson clock.
15. _____ Forum souvenir/program stand.
16. _____ Stanley Cup banner 1992–93.
17. _____ Clarence Campbell's seat.
18. _____ Honours Board of past Canadiens greats, from the Canadiens' dressing room.

3

TITANS OF THE TWINE

In describing his profession, goalie Gerry Cheevers said it best: "A baseball catcher's job is the closest thing to it. I mean, he alone dons the tools of ignorance and crouches behind the plate like an orangutan. But even the catcher goes up to hit like the rest of the ballplayers. So we goaltenders, alone and unloved, tend to very proud bastards."

Puck stoppers have always been among an elite: the proud few who are both crazy and fearless. In this chapter, we showcase the heroic exploits of these titans of the twine.

(Answers are on page 30)

3.1 **Which goalie owns the rare distinction of having been nominated for the rookie-of-the-year award in two different leagues in the same season?**
A. Jim Carey
B. Mike Richter
C. Patrick Roy
D. Curtis Joseph

3.2 **Which goalie won the Vezina Trophy as the NHL's top netminder straight out of high school?**
A. Ron Hextall
B. Tom Barrasso
C. Mike Richter
D. Jim Carey

3.3 When Grant Fuhr started his 76th game on March 31, 1996, he broke whose record for most games played by a goalie in a season?
A. His own record
B. Ed Belfour's record
C. Sean Burke's record
D. Arturs Irbe's record

3.4 Who is the youngest goalie to record 300 NHL wins?
A. Patrick Roy
B. Terry Sawchuk
C. Tony Esposito
D. Harry Lumley

3.5 Who earned the moniker "Mr. Zero" by beginning his NHL career with six shutouts in his first eight games?
A. Turk Broda
B. Frank Brimsek
C. Bill Durnan
D. Chuck Rayner

3.6 Which horror movie did Vancouver Canucks goalie Corey Hirsch salute with the mask he wore in 1995–96?
A. *Dracula*
B. *Psycho*
C. *Friday the 13th*
D. *The Phantom of the Opera*

3.7 In 1995–96, which French netminder donned a new mask, with artwork that paid tribute to Jacques Plante?
A. Guy Hebert
B. Patrick Roy
C. Martin Brodeur
D. Jocelyn Thibault

3.8 In 1954, Chicago Blackhawks goalie Al Rollins won the Hart Trophy as the NHL's MVP. There were several unusual aspects to Rollins's triumph. Which of the following is *not* one of them?
A. He played for a last-place club
B. He failed to make the First or Second All-Star Team
C. He was the first goalie to win the MVP award
D. He had the league's worst goals-against average

3.9 Which goalkeeper backed up Ken Dryden and Tony Esposito on Team Canada during the 1972 Summit Series?
A. Doug Favell
B. Jim Rutherford
C. Eddie Johnston
D. Cesare Maniago

3.10 Which team hired former Soviet star Vladislav Tretiak as a goaltending coach in 1990?
A. The New Jersey Devils
B. The Montreal Canadiens
C. The Buffalo Sabres
D. The Chicago Blackhawks

3.11 When Chris Osgood fired the puck into an empty Hartford Whalers net on March 6, 1996, he became the third NHL netminder credited with a goal. This was actually the second time Osgood had scored an empty-net goal. Where did he score the other one?
A. In Canadian junior hockey
B. In the American Hockey League
C. In the International Hockey League
D. In American college hockey

3.12 Who posted the NHL's best save percentage in 1995–96?
A. Toronto's Felix Potvin
B. Buffalo's Dominik Hasek
C. New Jersey's Martin Brodeur
D. Tampa Bay's Daren Puppa

3.13 Which Hall of Fame goalie was never elected to either the First or Second NHL All-Star Team during his career?
A. Ed Giacomin
B. Gump Worsley
C. Billy Smith
D. Gerry Cheevers

3.14 When asked why he didn't wear a mask, who replied: "My face is my mask."?
A. Johnny Bower
B. Glenn Hall
C. Turk Broda
D. Gump Worsley

3.15 In 1928–29, Montreal Canadiens goalie George Hainsworth registered an NHL-record 22 shutouts in a 44-game schedule. How many games did the Habs win that season?
A. 22
B. 26
C. 30
D. 34

3.16 Which team selected Ken Dryden in the 1964 amateur draft, only to later trade his rights to Montreal?
A. The Boston Bruins
B. The Detroit Red Wings
C. The Chicago Blackhawks
D. The Toronto Maple Leafs

TITANS OF THE TWINE
Answers

3.1 A. Jim Carey
In 1994–95, the "Net Detective" was nominated for rookie-of-the year honours in two different leagues in the same season. Carey's performance in 55 games with the AHL's Portland Pirates won him the Dudley "Red" Garrett Memorial Trophy as the league's top freshman. His sparkling netminding in 28 games (18–6–3 and a 2.13 GAA) after being called up by the Washington Capitals also made him a finalist in the balloting for the NHL's Calder Trophy, which was won by high-scoring centre Peter Forsberg.

3.2 B. Tom Barrasso
The 18-year-old Barrasso had a remarkable rookie season in 1983–84. He joined the Buffalo Sabres right out of Massachusetts' Acton-Boxboro high school and captured the Vezina with a 2.84 GAA. As if that wasn't enough, he also won the Calder Trophy as top rookie and was elected to the First All-Star Team.

3.3 A. His own record
When Fuhr started his 76th game for the St. Louis Blues on March 31, 1996, he broke his own NHL record for games played by a goalie in one season: 75, set in 1987–88 with the Edmonton Oilers. Fuhr injured his knee in his 77th game, thwarting his bid to start all 82 games of the 1995–96 schedule, although he did return to play two more games before the season's end. The last goalie to suit up for every game in a season was Eddie Johnston, who played every minute of the 70-game 1963–64 campaign with the Boston Bruins. (Interestingly, Martin Brodeur and Bill Ranford also broke Fuhr's old record in 1995–96, when both netminders made 77 appearances between the pipes.)

Most Regular-Season Games by a Goalie*

Player	Team	GP	Year
Grant Fuhr	St. Louis	79	1995-96
Martin Brodeur	New Jersey	77	1995-96
Bill Ranford	Edm/Bos	77	1995-96
Grant Fuhr	Edmonton	75	1987-88
Ed Belfour	Chicago	74	1990-91
Arturs Irbe	San Jose	74	1993-94
Current to 1996.			

3.4   B. Terry Sawchuk
The NHL's all-time victory leader was two months past his 30th birthday when he won his 300th game with the Detroit Red Wings in 1960. Roy was just one month older than Sawchuk when he posted win number 300 with the Colorado Avalanche on February 19, 1996.

3.5   B. Frank Brimsek
Boston fans were upset when Bruins manager Art Ross sold Tiny Thompson, the team's All-Star goalie, to the Detroit Red Wings for $15,000 early in the 1938–39 season. But they soon forgave Ross when Thompson's replacement, American-born Frank Brimsek, posted six shutouts in his first eight games and set a new Bruins record for scoreless minutes with a string of 231 minutes 54 seconds of flawless goaltending. Brimsek was hailed as "Mr. Zero," a title he lived up to by winning the Vezina Trophy as the NHL's top netminder with a stingy 1.58 goals-against average and a league-high 10 shutouts. Brimsek topped off his brilliant rookie season by backstopping the Bruins to the regular-season title and a Stanley Cup championship.

3.6   B. *Psycho*
Hirsch is a flaky character, so it's not surprising that his choice of mask artwork should be unusual. Artist

Frank Cipra adorned Hirsch's headgear with a painted replica of the Bates's manor from the Alfred Hitchcock horror classic, *Psycho*.

3.7   D. Jocelyn Thibault

Thibault's mask in 1995–96 sported an illustrated reproduction of the front of one of Jacques Plante's early goalie masks. The idea of honouring the former Montreal great came not from Thibault, but from artist Michel Lefebvre, to whom Thibault gave carte blanche to design the mask how he liked. As Lefebvre noted: "It's about time someone paid tribute to Plante and what he did for goalies."

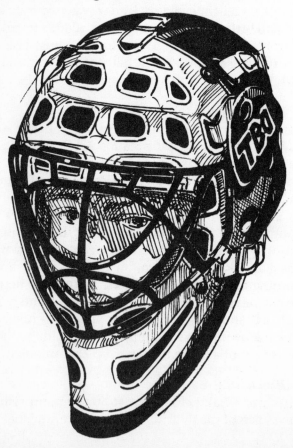

3.8   C. He was the first goalie to win the MVP award
Rollins was the third netminder to claim the coveted
Hart Trophy, but he is arguably the most unlikely selection ever. It is hard to imagine a goalie winning MVP
honours with a last-place team under any circum-
stances, but to do it with the 1953–54 Blackhawks is
mind-boggling. Chicago lost 51 games in 1953–54, a
record low for a 70-game schedule, and finished a
whopping 37 points behind the fifth-place Rangers.
Rollins won the Hart despite posting a 3.23 GAA, the
worst in the league. Amazingly, he was ignored in the
All-Star voting. The first- and second-team selections
were Harry Lumley and Terry Sawchuk.

3.9   C. Eddie Johnston
Johnston was the odd man out for Team Canada in the
1972 showdown. Relegated to bench duty behind Ken
Dryden and Tony Esposito, he did not appear in any of
the eight games against the Soviets. Johnston accepted
his situation without complaining. As he noted, "I was
just happy to be picked for the series."

3.10 D. The Chicago Blackhawks
Although it was the Montreal Canadiens who secured
Tretiak's playing rights by drafting him 138th in the
1983 entry draft, his eventual passport into the NHL
would be as a goaltending consultant with Chicago in
1990. Tretiak's first assignment was tutoring the
Hawks' rookie netminder, Ed Belfour. Tretiak clearly
had an impact. In 1990–91, Belfour claimed the Vezina
Trophy as top netminder, the Jennings Trophy for allowing the fewest goals and the Calder Trophy as outstanding rookie.

3.11 A. In Canadian junior hockey
Dead-eye Osgood also scored a goal for the Medicine
Hat Tigers during a Western Canadian Junior League
game against the Swift Current Broncos in 1991. Ironi-

cally, Hartford Whalers left-winger Geoff Sanderson, a graduate of the Broncos, was on the ice as an opponent for both of Osgood's markers.

3.12 B. Buffalo's Dominik Hasek

Hasek may possess the most unorthodox style of any NHL netminder, but he gets the job done. For the third season in a row, "the Dominator" led the NHL in save percentage. The Buffalo Sabres goalie stopped 92 per cent of the shots he faced in 1995–96.

Save-Percentage Leaders 1995-96					
Goalie	**Team**	**GP**	**GA**	**Shots**	**Pct.**
Dominik Hasek	Buf	59	161	2011	.920
Daren Puppa	TB	57	131	1605	.918
Jeff Hackett	Chi	35	80	948	.916
Guy Hebert	Ana	59	157	1820	.914
Ron Hextall	Phi	53	112	1292	.913
Mike Richter	NYR	41	107	1221	.912

3.13 D. Gerry Cheevers

Not only was Cheevers never named to an All-Star team during his 13-year NHL career, he never won any kind of individual award. Although Cheesie's stats may not have been as impressive as the Drydens and Parents of his era, he was a fierce competitor and a proven winner. As Boston general manager Harry Sinden once noted about Cheevers: "Gerry would throw his head in the way of the puck in order to stop a shot." Cheevers still owns the longest undefeated streak by a netminder: 32 games (24 wins/eight ties) with Boston in 1971–72. Known as a "money goalie," he could be counted on to come through in the clutch. He won Stanley Cups with Boston in 1970 and 1972.

3.14 D. Gump Worsley

Gump was as quick with a quip as he was with his catching glove. Despite receiving facial cuts requiring more than 200 stitches, Worsley resisted donning a mask until 1973–74, the final season of his 21-year career.

3.15 A. 22

Believe it or not, Montreal managed only 22 wins, despite Hainsworth's 22 shutouts and a microscopic 0.98 goals-against average. The explanation? Scoring slumped to an all-time low in 1928–29. Teams averaged a paltry 1.45 goals per game and the eight NHL clubs combined for 120 shutouts. Eighteen of Montreal's wins came via shutouts and the club was involved in four 0–0 ties. In an effort to open up the game, the league eliminated restrictions on forward passing the next season. It worked: the number of shutouts dropped to 26 and Hainsworth recorded only four.

3.16 A. The Boston Bruins

Dryden, who played Junior B hockey in Toronto, was Boston's third pick, 14th overall, in the NHL's draft of unsigned juniors in June 1964. For Dryden, who was an ardent Bruins fan as a boy, it was a dream come true. But after the draft Boston made a monumental gaffe when they traded Dryden and Alex Campbell to Montreal in exchange for the rights to Guy Allen and Paul Reid. Boston discovered the enormity of its mistake in the 1971 playoffs, when Dryden's miraculous goaltending helped Montreal upset the heavily-favoured Bruins in the quarterfinals. Dryden went on to lead the Habs to the Stanley Cup that year, his first of six Cups in his brief eight-year career.

GAME 3

TILL THE FAT LADY SINGS

In this game, we pull out all the stops and take your game to the next level by feathering a few cliches to the open man crashing the net. It's time to dig deep. Stay out of the box and complete these well-worn hockey phrases.

(Solutions are on page 113)

"Take your game . . ."	" . . . with a suspension."
"Stay . . ."	" . . . till the fat lady sings."
"He's a future . . ."	" . . . fair market value."
"Defense . . ."	" . . . team effort."
"Push your opponents . . ."	" . . . your injuries."
"He scored one . . ."	" . . . at a time."
"He kept his team . . ."	" . . . for an undisclosed amount."
"He threaded the puck . . ."	" . . . every shift."
"Enforcers . . ."	" . . . if you don't score."
"There's . . ."	" . . . to make the play."
"He instigated an altercation . . ."	" . . . and act as a third defenseman."

1. "I just give 110 per cent _____."

2. " _____ right on the tape."

3. "He signed a multiyear deal _____."

4. "The game ain't over _____."

5. " _____ to the next level."

36

6. "＿＿＿＿＿＿ focussed."

7. " Goalies clear the loose rubber ＿＿＿＿＿＿＿＿＿＿＿＿.

8. " In the deal, he got ＿＿＿＿＿＿＿＿."

9. "＿＿＿＿＿＿＿＿ in the game."

10. "It's a total ＿＿＿＿＿＿＿＿＿＿＿＿＿＿."

11. " ＿＿＿＿＿＿＿＿＿ through the five-hole."

12. "They take the check ＿＿＿＿＿＿＿＿＿."

13. " ＿＿＿＿＿＿ answer the bell."

14. "You can't win ＿＿＿＿＿＿＿＿＿＿."

15. " ＿＿＿＿＿＿＿ Hall-of-Famer."

16. "You gotta play through ＿＿＿＿＿＿＿＿."

17. "He was slapped ＿＿＿＿＿＿＿＿＿＿＿."

18. " ＿＿＿＿＿＿＿＿＿ to the brink."

19. " ＿＿＿＿＿＿＿ wins championships."

20. "Take it one shift ＿＿＿＿＿＿＿＿＿."

21. " ＿＿＿＿＿＿ no tomorrow."

22. " ＿＿＿＿＿＿＿＿＿ and was called on the carpet."

4

WHO AM I?

"I was the last Winnipeg Jet to score a goal in the club's 17-year history. *Who Am I?*" In this chapter, we alter the game tempo, still providing multiple-choice answers but in a different format. Listed below are 24 players. Match 16 of them to the following *Who Am I?* quotes. To settle our first question: Winnipeg defenseman Norm Maciver popped the Jets' final goal on April 28, 1996. The 4–1 loss to Detroit in the first round of the Western Conference playoffs was the last Jets game played in the Manitoba city.

(Answers are on page 40)

Brad Park	Bobby Hull	Bill Gadsby
Steve Shutt	Nels Stewart	Alex Delvecchio
Bobby Smith	Val Fonteyne	Marcel Dionne
Roy Conacher	Joe Primeau	Max Bentley
Ken Morrow	Eddie Shore	Pierre Larouche
Rick Martin	Howie Morenz	Babe Pratt
Doug Harvey	Frank Boucher	Gordie Drillon
Johnny Bucyk	Tom Johnson	Rick MacLeish

4.1 I am the only player to win the Norris Trophy as the NHL's top defenseman in the same year I was a playing coach. *Who am I?*

4.2 In 1969, I became the third player in NHL annals to compile 1,000 career points. *Who am I?*

4.3 I am the first left-winger in NHL history to score 60 goals in a season. *Who am I?*

4.4 Although both Wayne Gretzky and Stan Mikita won the NHL scoring title and the Lady Byng Trophy as most gentlemanly player in the same year, I was the first NHLer to do it. *Who am I?*

4.5 I am the first player to post 50-goal seasons for two NHL teams. *Who am I?*

4.6 I was drafted fourth overall by Boston in the 1970 amateur draft. The Bruins later traded me to Philadelphia, a move they had reason to regret when I netted the only goal in the Flyers' 1–0 Stanley Cup-clinching victory over Boston in game six of the 1974 finals. *Who am I?*

4.7 In the last year of my career, I negotiated a unique contract that allowed me to play with a team in the American Hockey League, as well as with my NHL club. *Who am I?*

4.8 I played on the first two New York Ranger Stanley Cup-winning teams in 1928 and 1933. In 1940, I coached the Rangers to a third Cup. I also won a record seven Lady Byng Trophies as the NHL's most gentlemanly player. *Who am I?*

4.9 I am the only defenseman to score three overtime goals in the Stanley Cup playoffs. *Who am I?*

4.10 Guy Lafleur and Marcel Dionne were picked ahead of me in the 1971 entry draft, but I outscored both of them in my first year. In fact, I was the first NHL rookie to break the 40-goal barrier. *Who am I?*

4.11 Fate wasn't kind to me. I was a runner-up in the voting for the Norris Trophy as the NHL's outstanding defenseman six times, and despite making the playoffs 17 times, I never won a Stanley Cup. *Who am I?*

4.12 Although I never won the Lady Byng Trophy as the league's most gentlemanly player, I am arguably the cleanest NHLer to lace up a pair of skates. I once played a record 185 games without earning a single penalty. *Who am I?*

4.13 I am the only rookie to win an NHL scoring crown. I was called "Old Poison" because of my lethal touch around the net. *Who am I?*

4.14 I played on six Stanley Cup winners with the Montreal Canadiens during my 15-year NHL career and I won the Norris Trophy as the league's top defenseman in 1959. I later coached the Boston Bruins to a Stanley Cup triumph in 1972. *Who am I?*

4.15 I scored more goals than my two older brothers, who, unlike me, are both in the Hall of Fame. Despite missing four seasons during World War II, I registered eight 20-goal seasons in the NHL. I won two Cups with Boston and captured a scoring title with Chicago. *Who am I?*

4.16 I outscored Wayne Gretzky to set an Ontario Junior A scoring record of 192 points in 1977–78. *Who am I?*

WHO AM I?
Answers

4.1 A mainstay of the Montreal Canadiens defense corps during the 1950s, **Doug Harvey** won his seventh

Norris Trophy as the NHL's best defenseman in 1960–61, while doing double duty as a playing coach with the New York Rangers. Under Harvey's stewardship, the Rangers made the playoffs for the first time in four years. Despite his success, Harvey quit his coaching post the next year, though he remained with the Blueshirts as a player for another two seasons. He disliked the isolation that came with coaching. "When I was a coach, I couldn't be one of the boys," he said. "This way if I want a beer with them, I get a beer."

4.2 On February 16, 1969, **Alex Delvecchio**, the man they called "Motor City Fats," became the third player in NHL annals to score 1,000 career points. The centre for Ted Lindsay and Gordie Howe on Detroit's famous Production Line in the 1950s, Delvecchio would play 24 years in the NHL and rack up 1,281 career points before finally hanging up the blades in 1974.

The NHL's First 1,000-Point Players			
Player	**Team**	**Date**	**Game No.**
Gordie Howe	Det	Nov/27/60	938
Jean Béliveau	Mtl	Mar/3/68	911
Alex Delvecchio	**Det**	**Feb/16/69**	**1143**
Bobby Hull	Chi	Dec/12/70	909
Norm Ullman	Tor	Oct/16/71	1113

4.3 The most dangerous scoring line of the Montreal Canadiens powerhouse of the late 1970s featured Jacques Lemaire at centre, Guy Lafleur on right wing and **Steve Shutt** on the left side. Although less spectacular than Lafleur, Shutt was just as deadly from the circles in. His 60-goal performance in 1976–77 set a new standard for left-wingers that would last 16 years, until Luc Robitaille scored 63 in 1992–93.

4.4 Although Wayne Gretzky and Stan Mikita each won the scoring title and the Lady Byng in one season (each did it twice!), the first player so honoured was right-winger **Gordie Drillon** of the 1937–38 Toronto Maple Leafs. Drillon nipped teammate Syl Apps for the scoring crown by two points and claimed the Lady Byng with just four penalty minutes.

4.5 **Pierre Larouche** looked to be headed for an awesome NHL career when he scored 53 goals and 58 assists for the Pittsburgh Penguins in his sophomore season in 1975–76. But he never quite lived up to the high expectations placed on him, despite hitting the 50-goal mark again with Montreal in 1979–80. Many hockey observers felt he simply didn't take the game seriously enough.

4.6 **Rick MacLeish** and teammate Reggie Leach, both former Boston Bruins, contributed mightily to the rise of the Philadelphia Flyers in the mid-1970s. But the trading of MacLeish, who led all playoff point scorers in both of the Flyers' two Cup-winning years, proved particularly galling to Boston. It was his goal (a deflection of Moose Dupont's point shot), that stood up as the winning margin as the Flyers muzzled the Bruins 1–0 to claim the Cup in six games in 1974.

4.7 In 1939, as he neared the end of his NHL career, **Eddie Shore** bought the AHL's Springfield Indians for $40,000. Aware that his presence in Springfield's lineup would be a great drawing card, Shore laced up for the Indians. Soon, Boston manager Art Ross came calling and struck a deal with Shore that would allow the veteran blueliner to play home games for both the Bruins and the Indians during the 1939–40 season. But Shore soon began itching to play in Springfield's road games as well, which prompted an exasperated Ross to trade his troublesome star to the New York Americans.

In one stretch that spring, Shore played eight games in eight nights, flying between various cities to maintain his commitments to both the Amerks and the Indians. He was 38 at the time.

4.8 One of the slickest playmaking centres of all time, **Frank Boucher** won a record seven Lady Byng Trophies as the NHL's most gentlemanly player in the eight years between 1928 and 1935. After he claimed the hardware for the seventh time, the NHL gave the award to Boucher to keep and a new trophy was donated by Lady Byng, the wife of Canada's then governor general, Lord Byng.

4.9 With a grand total of only 17 regular-season goals in his 10-year NHL career, defenseman **Ken Morrow** was no sniper, but the New York Islanders rearguard had a knack for scoring crucial goals in the spring. He notched 11 goals in 127 post-season games, and potted sudden-death winners three times: against the Los Angeles Kings in 1980, against the Edmonton Oilers in 1981 and against the New York Rangers in 1984.

4.10 The left-winger on the Buffalo Sabres' famed French Connection Line, **Rick Martin** had the heavy shot and soft hands of a natural goal scorer. While first-pick Lafleur scored 29 goals and second-pick Dionne, 28 goals, Martin (fifth pick overall) blew an NHL rookie-record 44 goals past opposition netminders in 1971–72. And Martin was just heating up. In both his third and fourth NHL campaigns he lit the lamp 52 times. Martin's career came to a premature end when he was forced to retire because of knee miseries in 1982. Had he played a few more years in good health, Martin would surely be a member of the Hall of Fame.

4.11 Timing was not on **Brad Park**'s side. He entered the NHL in 1968–69, just as Bobby Orr was in the process of making the Norris Trophy (top NHL defenseman) his own private possession. Park placed second to Orr in the Norris balloting four times. After Orr's gimpy knees forced him to retire in 1978–79, Park found himself twice more the bridesmaid in Norris voting to two other future Hall-of-Famers, Denis Potvin and Larry Robinson, who split the award for the next five years. Despite surgery-scarred knees of his own, Park lasted 17 seasons in the NHL, qualifying for the playoffs each year but never skating on a Cup winner.

4.12 A steady journeyman who spent most of his NHL career in Detroit and Pittsburgh, **Val Fonteyne** took only 13 minor penalties and not a single major penalty in 820 regular-season NHL games, and just two minors in 149 WHA games. During one stretch Fonteyne played 185 straight games without committing a foul. The streak began when Fonteyne was with Detroit. He took a minor in a game against Montreal on February 28, 1965, and did not visit the penalty box again until December 1, 1968, when he was with Pittsburgh. Fonteyne's next cleanest streak, 157 games, is the second longest in NHL history.

4.13 As the triggerman on the Montreal Maroons' "S" Line with Hooley Smith and Babe Siebert in the late 1920s and early 1930s, **Nels Stewart** displayed a deadly touch around the net. "Old Poison" owned the NHL career-scoring record of 324 goals until Rocket Richard surpassed it in 1952–53. But no one has ever equalled another of Stewart's scoring benchmarks: leading the NHL in scoring as a rookie. In his freshman season, in 1925–26, he tallied 34 goals and eight assists, six points better than Cy Denneny of the Ottawa Senators. Only one other first-year player has topped the NHL's point parade: Joe Malone, in 1917–18. But no one in the league was classified as a rookie that season since it was the NHL's first year of operation.

4.14 Blueliner **Tom Johnson** played in the very large shadow of Doug Harvey on the great Montreal Canadiens teams of the 1950s. Only once did Johnson emerge into the spotlight, when he won the Norris Trophy as top D-man in 1958–59, snapping Harvey's stranglehold on the award. After his playing days ended, Johnson added another Stanley Cup ring to his collection by coaching the Big Bad Bruins to the winner's circle in 1972.

4.15 It is a clear injustice that **Roy Conacher** isn't in the Hall of Fame with his older brothers, Charlie and Lionel. Roy outscored both of his more famous siblings during his career and posted eight 20-goal NHL seasons during a time when that really meant something. In fact, Conacher registered more 20-goal seasons than any player of his era except for the great Rocket Richard. Conacher's stats would have been even more impressive had he not spent nearly four years when he was at his prime in the armed forces during World War II. Even so, at age 32, he proved he still had plenty of gas left in his tank when he won the scoring crown with Chicago in 1948–49.

4.16 In 1977–78, 20-year-old **Bobby Smith** of the Ottawa 67s waged a year-long battle with 17-year-old rookie Wayne Gretzky of the Sault Ste. Marie Greyhounds for the Ontario Hockey Association scoring title. When the smoke finally cleared, Smith had bested Gretzky by 10 points, 192 to 182. Smith would enjoy a distinguished 16-year NHL career with the Minnesota North Stars and Montreal Canadiens, but he never outpointed the Great One again.

GAME 4

BEHIND THE MASK

It was the Rangers' Mike Richter who once said: "Playing in net is like playing golf. You play against yourself. You know when you're not playing good or you've missed a shot. The true measure of a goalie is how consistent he is." Usually, it's what goes on behind the mask that makes the big difference in performance.

The 59 goalies listed below have all experienced the odd off-night. Their names appear in the puzzle horizontally, vertically, diagonally or backwards. Some are easily found, like Grant F-U-H-R, others require a more careful search. After you've circled all 59 names, read the remaining letters in descending order to spell the name of the goaltender whose "scarred" mask is featured in our puzzle drawing.

(Solutions are on page 114)

BARRASSO	BEAUPRE	BELFOUR	BENEDICT
BLUE	BERTHIAUME	BOWER	BRODA
BURKE	CASEY	CHABOT	CHEVELDAE
CROZIER	DRYDEN	DURNAN	ESPOSITO
ESSENSA	FITZPATRICK	FISET	FRANCIS
FUHR	GARDINER	GIACOMIN	HACKETT
HALL	HASEK	HAYWARD	HEALY
HEXTALL	HIRSCH	HODGE	HOLMES
IRBE	JABLONSKI	KERR	LINDBERGH
KIDD	LIUT	LOW	MALARCHUK
MCCOOL	MELOCHE	MIO	MOOG
MYRE	OSGOOD	PARENT	POTVIN
RAYNER	RANFORD	REESE	RESCH
RICHTER	ROY	SMITH	TERRERI
THOMPSON	WORSLEY	WREGGET	

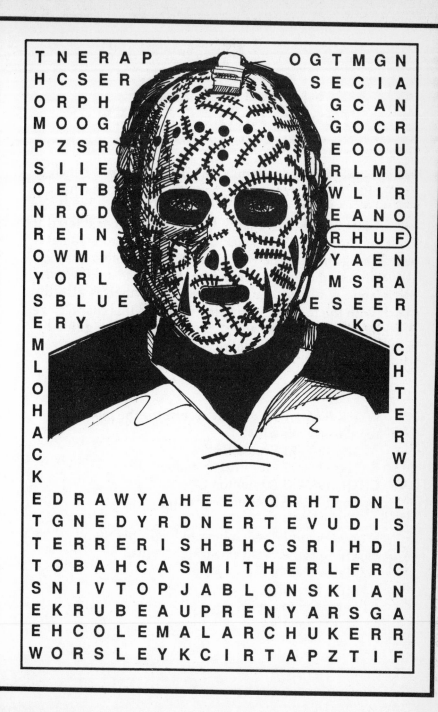

```
T N E R A P        O G T M G N
H C S E R          S E C I A
O R P H G          G C A C R
M O O G R          G O C O U
P Z S I E B        E O L M D I
S I I T D          R L I R
O E T O B I        W E A N O
N R O D I N        E (R H U F)
R E I N I L        Y A E N A
O W M I L          M S R
Y O R L U E        E S E E R
S B L U E          K C
E R Y
M                                    R
L                                    I
O                                    C
H                                    H
A                                    T
C                                    E
K                                    R
E                                    W
T                                    O
T                                    L
S                                    S
E                                    I
    E D R A W Y A H E E X O R H T D N L
    T G N E D Y R D N E R T E V U D I S
    T E R R E R I S H B H C S R I H D I
    T O B A H C A S M I T H E R L F R C
    S N I V T O P J A B L O N S K I A N
    E K R U B E A U P R E N Y A R S G A
    E H C O L E M A L A R C H U K E R R
    W O R S L E Y K C I R T A P Z T I F
```

47

5

TEAMS AND COACHES

When Scotty Bowman stepped behind the Detroit bench to battle the Dallas Stars on December 29, 1995, he was making NHL history. Bowman, in his 1,607th match, set a new league record for most games coached. Although he considered it "just another game," Bowman's accomplishment is remarkable. Along the way, he was a trailblazer for other coaches, being among the first to move from team to team. Five NHL clubs and six Stanley Cup titles later, Bowman is also the coach with the most wins in NHL history. In this chapter, we champion bench bosses and the teams they have guided—both the great and the ordinary.

(Answers are on page 51)

5.1 **Which team owns the NHL record for the most regular-season wins?**
A. The 1970–71 Boston Bruins
B. The 1976–77 Montreal Canadiens
C. The 1983–84 Edmonton Oilers
D. The 1995–96 Detroit Red Wings

5.2 **Who is the only bench boss to begin his NHL coaching career with six straight wins?**
A. Mario Tremblay
B. Mike Keenan
C. Larry Robinson
D. Marc Crawford

5.3 Which club was dubbed "Team Concussion" in 1995–96?
A. The Ottawa Senators
B. The San Jose Sharks
C. The New York Islanders
D. The Toronto Maple Leafs

5.4 Which coach said after losing his job in 1995–96, "I had never even been fired from a paper route."?
A. Rick Ley
B. Pat Burns
C. Jacques Demers
D. Kevin Constantine

5.5 Which team was named after a restaurant?
A. The Calgary Flames
B. The New York Rangers
C. The Chicago Blackhawks
D. The Tampa Bay Lightning

5.6 Which team's owners were infuriated when sportswriters nicknamed the club's new $160-million arena, "the Garage"?
A. The Vancouver Canucks'
B. The Ottawa Senators'
C. The Boston Bruins'
D. The Chicago Blackhawks'

5.7 Detroit had two other names before becoming the Red Wings. What were they?
A. The Blades and the Racers
B. The Maroons and the Tigers
C. The Bulldogs and the Cyclones
D. The Falcons and the Cougars

5.8 Mario Lemieux, Jaromir Jagr and Ron Francis of the Pittsburgh Penguins missed ranking 1–2–3 in the NHL scoring derby in 1995–96, when Joe Sakic edged Francis by one point. Which was the last team to have three players finish 1–2–3 in scoring?
A. The 1949–50 Detroit Red Wings
B. The 1966–67 Chicago Blackhawks
C. The 1973–74 Boston Bruins
D. The 1986–87 Edmonton Oilers

5.9 Which team's logo did broadcaster Don Cherry derisively describe as looking like "a condom package"?
A. The New York Islanders
B. The Ottawa Senators
C. The Colorado Avalanche
D. The Los Angeles Kings

5.10 Which NHL coach was criticizing Wayne Gretzky when he said: "You have to expect your best players to carry the team and that's not happening."
A. Glen Sather
B. Larry Robinson
C. Mike Keenan
D. Barry Melrose

5.11 "Take the shortest route to the puck—and arrive in ill humour," was which coach's advice on how to play hockey?
A. Fred Shero's
B. Al Arbour's
C. Harry Neale's
D. Punch Imlach's

5.12 Since the creation of the NHL in 1917–18, how many Stanley-Cup winning coaches have scored Stanley Cup-winning goals?
A. Two
B. Four
C. Six
D. It has never happened

5.13 Who is the only NHL coach to be fired and then re-hired by the same team two days later?
A. Don Cherry
B. Butch Goring
C. Michel Bergeron
D. Roger Neilson

5.14 What is the title of Mike Keenan's favourite book?
A. *War and Peace*
B. *The Great Gatsby*
C. *Heart of Darkness*
D. *The Right Stuff*

5.15 Which coach introduced "pyramid power" to the NHL?
A. Barry Melrose
B. Herb Brooks
C. Phil Maloney
D. Red Kelly

TEAMS AND COACHES
Answers

5.1 D. The 1995–96 Detroit Red Wings
The Red Wings' juggernaut steamrolled everything in

its path during the 1995–96 regular season. Not only did Detroit set a new NHL record with 62 wins, the club also finished first in goals against, first in penalty killing, third in goals scored and third in power play percentage. Detroit was so dominant, many wondered if this was the best team in NHL history. Wings coach Scotty Bowman, who also coached the Montreal squads that posted the second-, third- and fourth-highest win totals of all time, refused to offer an opinion. A few weeks later, when Detroit was rudely knocked out of the playoffs by the Colorado Avalanche, the debate lost its steam. Each of Bowman's Montreal powerhouses won the Stanley Cup, something a team must do to be considered the all-time best.

The NHL's All-Time Regular-Season Win Leaders

Year	Team	GP	W	L	T	PTS
1995-96	Detroit Red Wings	82	62	13	7	131
1976-77	Montreal Canadiens	80	60	8	12	132
1977-78	Montreal Canadiens	80	59	10	11	129
1975-76	Montreal Canadiens	80	58	11	11	127
1970-71	Boston Bruins	78	57	14	7	121
1983-84	Edmonton Oilers	80	57	18	5	119

5.2 A. Mario Tremblay
Who says you need experience? Despite having never coached before at any level of pro hockey, Mario Tremblay earned a spot in the record books when Montreal defeated Boston 3–1 on October 31, 1995. The victory was Tremblay's sixth in a row, the longest winning streak at the start of an NHL coaching career. The previous mark of five was set by Bep Guidolin of the Bruins in 1973, and was equalled by Marc Crawford of the Quebec Nordiques in 1994.

5.3   C. The New York Islanders
There was a disturbingly high number of concussions in the NHL in 1995–96, but no team suffered as many as the Islanders, who lost seven players with head injuries: Brett Lindros, Dennis Vaske, Todd Bertuzzi, Ken Belanger, Dean Chynoweth, Derek King and Zigmund Palffy. The most serious concussion was sustained by Lindros, who, at age 20, was forced to retire.

5.4   B. Pat Burns
When the Maple Leafs fell into a 3–16–3 tailspin and looked in danger of not making the playoffs in 1995–96, Toronto general manager Cliff Fletcher reluctantly gave Burns his walking papers. It was a big comedown for the former two-time NHL coach-of-the-year, who had been the toast of the town a few years earlier after he guided the Leafs to two Conference finals.

5.5   C. The Chicago Blackhawks
When the Pacific Coast Hockey Association folded in 1926, one of its teams, the Portland Rosebuds, was purchased by Major Frederic McLaughlin (a Chicago aristocrat whose family had made millions in the coffee business). As Dick Irvin notes in his book *Behind the Bench*, the major owned a restaurant in Chicago called the Blackhawk, named after a military regiment he had commanded in World War I. Seeing a chance to grab a free plug for his eatery, McLaughlin gave his new hockey team the same name.

5.6   A. The Vancouver Canucks
The Vancouver sports press hung the blue-collar moniker "the Garage" on General Motors Place shortly after the $160-million, state-of-the-art stadium opened in September 1995. Officials from Orca Bay Sports and Entertainment, the company that owns both the Canucks and the arena, were not amused when use of the term became commonplace with radio and TV stations,

and even the national media. Neither was General Motors, who had paid millions of dollars for the right to name the arena.

5.7   D. The Falcons and the Cougars

Detroit entered the NHL in 1926–27 with a nucleus of players purchased from the Victoria Cougars of the defunct PCHA. The club retained the name Cougars until 1930–31, when it was changed to the Falcons. When James Norris, Sr. bought the franchise in 1932, he changed its name to the Red Wings and had a new logo designed—a winged wheel—inspired by the crest of a Montreal hockey team, the Winged Wheelers, he'd played on as a youth. It was a perfect fit for a team in an automotive town like Detroit.

5.8   C. The 1973–74 Boston Bruins

The swashbuckling Bruins of the late 1960s and early 1970s didn't just defeat their opponents, they demolished them with relentless waves of offense from the era's top goal scorers and playmakers. Playing a fullbore, pedal-to-the metal offensive style, Boston racked up the most goals in the NHL for seven straight seasons from 1967–68 to 1973–74. The Bruins so dominated the scoring sheets that in two seasons, 1970–71 and 1973–74, they boasted not only the league's top three point getters but also the top four, a feat no other team has duplicated. The club's big four in 1973–74 were Phil Esposito (145), Bobby Orr (119), Ken Hodge (105) and Wayne Cashman (89).

5.9   B. The Ottawa Senators

In adopting the name the Senators, Ottawa was tipping its hat to tradition. The original Ottawa Senators won nine Stanley Cups between 1903 and 1927, before relocating to St. Louis in 1934. Still, the choice of a helmeted Roman centurion for the team's emblem was peculiar, as it had little in common with either the original Senators or Roman statesmen. In typical bombastic fashion, Don Cherry used his soapbox on CBC's *Hockey Night in Canada* to compare the Senators' new logo to "a condom package." Presumably, Grapes was referring to Trojan-brand prophylactics.

5.10 C. Mike Keenan
During the 1996 Detroit-St. Louis Western Conference semifinals, Keenan publicly questioned Gretzky's performance, saying, among other things, "If he's not injured, then something must be bothering him." Keenan also berated the Great One in front of his teammates, which left Oilers general manager Glen Sather to muse: "I think (Keenan) should have his head examined. As far as I'm concerned he must be touched by the wind or something to be critical of a guy like Wayne Gretzky." Later, Keenan apologized to Gretzky, saying he may have "overstepped" himself in his comments.

5.11 A. Fred Shero's
Shero put his search-and-destroy coaching philosophy into action during his reign at the helm of the Philadelphia Flyers in the 1970s. Led by such menacing thugs as Dave "the Hammer" Schultz, Andre "Moose" Dupont and Bob "Hound Dog" Kelly, the Broad Street Bullies perfected the art of strategic intimidation and became the first post–1967 expansion team to win the Stanley Cup. In response to critics who accused the Flyers of playing too violently, Shero said: "If you keep the opposition on their butts, they don't score goals. If you want to see pretty skating, go to the Ice Capades."

5.12 B. Four
As of 1996, only four NHLers have scored a Stanley Cup-winning goal and also coached a Stanley Cup-winning team. The first to do it was Cy Denneny, who scored the Cup winner for Ottawa in 1927 and coached the Boston Bruins to the 1929 Cup; Frank Boucher of

the New York Rangers notched the Cup winner in 1928 and later coached the Rangers to the title in 1940; Toe Blake potted Cup winners in 1944 and 1946 and won eight Cups as a coach between 1956 and 1968 with the Canadiens; and Jacques Lemaire netted Cup-winning goals for Montreal in 1977 and 1979 and won the 1995 Stanley Cup as bench boss of the New Jersey Devils.

5.13 D. Roger Neilson

Fittingly, the man who has coached the most NHL teams is also the only coach to be fired and rehired in a span of two days. Following a Thursday night loss to Montreal in 1979, Neilson was abruptly dismissed by Toronto Maple Leafs owner Harold Ballard. But on Saturday, with a game against Philadelphia looming and the club unable to find anyone willing to take the job, Ballard reversed his decision and rehired Neilson. To milk the maximum publicity value out of the mystery of who would be the Leafs' new coach, Ballard asked Neilson to walk out behind the bench wearing a paper bag over his head, then dramatically remove it before the opening face-off. Neilson wisely refused. When he appeared, the hometown fans gave him a long ovation. But the reprieve was short-lived. Ballard gassed Neilson at the end of the season, this time for good.

5.14 B. *The Great Gatsby*

In a May 1995 *Sports Illustrated* article, writer Gary Smith reported that Mike Keenan keeps a well-worn copy of F. Scott Fitzgerald's novel *The Great Gatsby* on his bookshelf. It is filled with sentences Keenan has underlined, as well as assorted notes he has scribbled in the margins. Smith says that Iron Mike has read the book five times and continues to flip through it for inspiration. We can only speculate how much Keenan identifies with the novel's central character, Jay

Gatsby, a mysterious and wealthy socialite with a shady past, who is obsessed with another man's wife.

5.15 D. Red Kelly

When Kelly coached the Toronto Maple Leafs he was always trying to dream up motivational gimmicks. During the 1976 playoffs, he introduced pyramid power. As Brian McFarlane notes in his book, *The Leafs*, Kelly had heard about the mystical powers associated with pyramids and ordered that a large one be suspended from the ceiling of the Leafs dressing room. Smaller pyramids were arranged beneath the team bench. If players sat beneath these triangles or even placed their sticks under them, Kelly insisted, they could tap into psychic energy sources. The players were sceptical, but when captain Darryl Sittler tried it and scored five times in an 8–5 romp over the Philadelphia Flyers, many of them jumped on the bandwagon. Kelly scrapped his pyramid scheme after the Flyers bounced the Leafs from the playoffs in seven games.

GAME 5

THE EVOLUTION OF AN NHL RECORD

Most hockey fans know who holds the NHL's single-season goal-scoring record. But who else set records in this category dating back to the league's first season, 1917–18? In this game, we trace the evolution of two NHL records—Part 1: Most goals, one season; and the much more challenging, Part 2: Most points, one season.

Match the NHL record holders and their corresponding totals in the two columns below with the seasons in which they set the record. For example, in Part 1 we note that Bobby Hull scored 50 goals in 1961–62. Fill in the blanks above Hull with the players who previously held the record for most goals in a season, and the blanks below his name with the players who later smashed Hull's mark. (Note: Some players break their own records.)

(Solutions are on page 115)

Part 1: Most Goals, One Season

Record Holders		Goals Scored		
Phil Esposito	Joe Malone	58	76	44
Bobby Hull	Wayne Gretzky	50	92	50
Maurice Richard	Bobby Hull	54		
Bernie Geoffrion				

Player	Goals	Season
1. _____	_____	1917–18
2. _____	_____	1944–45
3. _____	_____	1960–61
4. Bobby Hull	50	1961–62
5. _____	_____	1965–66

6. _____	_____	1968–69
7. _____	_____	1970–71
8. _____	_____	1981–82

Part 2: Most Points, One Season

Record Holders

			Points Scored		
Wayne Gretzky	Joe Malone	Dickie Moore	44	48	51
Herb Cain	Phil Esposito	Gordie Howe	73	73	82
Bobby Hull	Doug Bentley	Joe Malone	95	96	97
Phil Esposito	Cooney Weiland	Stan Mikita	97	126	152
Howie Morenz	Wayne Gretzky		212	215	

Player	Points	Season
1. _____	_____	1917–18
2. _____	_____	1919–20
3. _____	_____	1927–28
4. _____	_____	1929–30
5. _____	_____	1942–43
6. _____	_____	1943–44
7. Gordie Howe	86	1950–51
8. _____	_____	1952–53
9. _____	_____	1958–59
10. _____	_____	1965–66
11. _____	_____	1966–67
12. _____	_____	1968–69
13. _____	_____	1970–71
14. _____	_____	1981–82
15. _____	_____	1985–86

6

ALL-STAR GAZING

Although representatives of the Professional Hockey Writers Association vote for the NHL's First and Second All-Star Teams, it's the hockey fans who determine the starting lineup at the annual All-Star game each January. The big question is: Which NHLer has attracted the most fan votes ever? In 1995–96, Paul Coffey collected 620,788 votes, the most by one player in the game's history. Now that we've given away that gem, what's left? Grab a ballot. We want your yeas and nays on an even better all-star lineup of questions about the NHL's best.

(Answers are on page 63)

6.1 **Which city hosted the NHL's first All-Star game?**
A. Boston
B. Montreal
C. Toronto
D. Ottawa

6.2 **What has yet to occur at an NHL All-Star game?**
A. A penalty-free game
B. A team posting a shutout
C. A player scoring seven points
D. A player receiving a major penalty for fighting

6.3 **Who is the only player to be voted to an NHL All-Star team after his death?**
A. Tim Horton
B. Babe Siebert
C. Howie Morenz
D. Pelle Lindbergh

6.4 How often did Gordie Howe and Wayne Gretzky appear together in an NHL All-Star game?
A. Never
B. Once
C. Twice
D. Three times

6.5 Who was dubbed "the Rodney Dangerfield of the NHL," when he was left off the roster for the 1996 NHL All-Star game?
A. Ron Francis
B. Alexei Zhamnov
C. John LeClair
D. Trevor Linden

6.6 The Fox network unveiled an electronic puck at the 1996 NHL All-Star game. What colour was the halo that surrounded the puck on TV screens?
A. Red
B. Blue
C. Green
D. Orange

6.7 What name did Fox give to its colour-enhanced puck?
A. FoxFire
B. FoxRay
C. FoxTrax
D. FoxGlow

6.8 Who was the first player to notch a hat trick in an NHL All-Star contest?
A. Ted Lindsay
B. Phil Esposito
C. Mike Bossy
D. Frank Mahovlich

6.9 Which goalie has earned the most NHL All-Star selections?
A. Glenn Hall
B. Ken Dryden
C. Jacques Plante
D. Terry Sawchuk

6.10 After winning an automobile for copping the MVP award at the 1989 NHL All-Star game, Wayne Gretzky announced he was giving his prize to someone else. Who?
A. His father, Walter
B. His wife, Janet
C. His agent, Michael Barnett
D. His former teammate, Dave Semenko

6.11 In 1978, the Campbell Conference All-Stars recorded the fewest shots on goal by a team in an NHL All-Star game. How many did the team collect?
A. 12
B. 16
C. 20
D. 24

6.12 When an injury forced Mark Messier to miss the 1993 All-Star game, which Ranger teammate replaced him and scored a record-tying four goals?
A. Adam Graves
B. Ed Olczyk
C. Mike Gartner
D. Tony Amonte

6.13 As of 1996, which NHL star has never been elected to the NHL's First or Second All-Star Team?
A. Steve Yzerman
B. Adam Oates
C. Dale Hawerchuk
D. Pat LaFontaine

6.14 Who was the first son to copy his father and play in an NHL All-Star game?
A. Mark Howe
B. Syl Apps, Jr.
C. Brett Hull
D. Tracy Pratt

6.15 Who holds the record for the most consecutive NHL First Team All-Star selections?
A. Bobby Hull
B. Doug Harvey
C. Bobby Orr
D. Wayne Gretzky

ALL-STAR GAZING
Answers

6.1 **C. Toronto**
Although there had been several previous benefit NHL All-Star contests, the first "official" NHL All-Star game was held in Toronto on October 13, 1947. A crowd of 14,138 gathered at Maple Leaf Gardens to watch the NHL All-Stars defeat the defending Stanley Cup-champion Maple Leafs 4–3. Doug Bentley of the Chicago Blackhawks scored the winning goal, drilling a shot past Turk Broda in the second minute of the third period. The inaugural game was both a financial and athletic success, but it was marred by an injury when Chicago's Bill Mosienko fractured his ankle after being checked into the boards.

6.2 **C. A player scoring seven points**
The record for points in an NHL All-Star game is six,

held by Mario Lemieux, who posted three goals and three assists in the 1988 tilt. There were no penalties called in 1992 and 1994; Charlie Hodge and Gary Bauman of the Montreal Canadiens combined to shutout the All-Stars 3–0 in 1967; and Gordie Howe received a major for fighting with Gus Mortson in the 1948 game.

6.3 D. Pelle Lindbergh

Early on a Sunday morning in November 1985, Philadelphia Flyers goalie Pelle Lindbergh lost control of his customized Porsche 930 Turbo on a sharp curve. The car skidded across the street, hit a curb and slammed into a wall. Lindbergh, who had been drinking, did not survive the crash. A day later, he was pronounced brain dead and disconnected from a life-support system in a New Jersey hospital. It was a tragic end to the 26-year-old's life and promising hockey career. The previous year, the Swedish-born Lindbergh had won the Vezina Trophy as the NHL's top netminder and was named to the First All-Star Team. In an emotional show of support, fans posthumously elected Lindbergh as the starting goalie for the Wales Conference team at the 1986 All-Star game in Hartford.

6.4 B. Once

The historic meeting occurred in 1980. Gretzky, a 19-year-old rookie, suited up for the Campbell Conference All-Stars, while the 51-year-old Howe, playing in his final NHL season after a six-year stint in the WHA, skated for the Wales Conference All-Stars. The game was held in Detroit, Howe's old stomping grounds, and he received a tremendous ovation from the Motown fans. Which of the two greats fared better in the game? Howe picked up an assist, while Gretzky was kept off the scoresheet.

6.5 A. Ron Francis

Even though Francis was off to the best season of his

career, he was not named to the roster of the Eastern Conference All-Stars by a selection committee of general managers. The slight prompted Pittsburgh's public relations office to compare Francis to Rodney Dangerfield, the comedian who "gets no respect." The Pens' centre did play in the game, however, but only after NHL commissioner Gary Bettman intervened on his behalf.

6.6 B. Blue

American audiences have long complained that they have problems following the fast-moving puck on television. The Fox network came up with a solution—a method of visually enhancing the puck with computer-generated graphics. The new gimmick was introduced at the 1996 NHL All-Star game, when viewers saw a shimmery, blue aura surrounding the puck. Whenever the disk reached speeds of 70 m.p.h or more, the colour turned to red and sprouted a fiery comet tail.

6.7 C. FoxTrax

In an effort to come up with a catchy moniker, the network dubbed its glowing puck FoxTrax. Its clever name aside, most hockey fans hated Fox's new innovation. In a *Hockey News* poll, 91 per cent of respondents gave the thumbs down to Fox's psychedelic puck effects, claiming they were an annoying distraction.

6.8 A. Ted Lindsay

Before a hometown crowd in 1950, Terrible Ted notched the first hat trick in All-Star competition, sparking the Red Wings to a 7–1 thumping of the All-Stars. Lindsay beat goalie Chuck Rayner of the New York Rangers 19 seconds after the opening face-off, then scored again with three minutes left in the first period before finally potting number three with five minutes left in the game.

6.9 A. Glenn Hall

He wasn't called "Mr. Goalie" for nothing. The acrobatic Hall garnered seven NHL First Team and four Second Team All-Star selections in an 18-year career split between Detroit, Chicago and St. Louis. Hall only played on one Cup winner, but no other goalie was ever as good for so long.

	Goalie All-Star Selections*			
Player	NHL Years	First Team	Second Team	Total
Glenn Hall	18	7	4	11
Frank Brimsek	10	2	6	8
Jacques Plante	18	3	4	7
Terry Sawchuk	21	3	4	7
Bill Durnan	7	6	0	6
Ken Dryden	8	5	1	6
*Current to 1996.				

6.10 D. His former teammate, Dave Semenko

The 1989 NHL All-Star game was held in Edmonton, and Wayne Gretzky, who had been traded to Los Angeles before the start of the season, celebrated his return to Northlands Coliseum by notching a goal and two assists and copping MVP honours. Afterwards, Gretzky surprised everyone, including the recently retired Semenko, by announcing he was giving the Dodge truck he had won as the game's MVP to his former Oiler teammate and on-ice protector.

6.11 A. 12

Despite a lineup that included Phil Esposito, Bobby Clarke, Bill Barber, Mike Bossy, Bryan Trottier and Denis Potvin, the Campbell Conference squad managed only a paltry 12 shots on net in three periods and nearly four minutes of overtime in the 1978 All-Star game. Even so, the Campbells nearly won the match, which was staged in Buffalo. They held a 2–1 lead until 18:21 of the third period, when the Sabres' Rick Martin knotted the score. The Wales Conference completed its comeback when another hometown hero, Gilbert Perreault, potted the winner in overtime.

6.12 C. Mike Gartner
Super-sub Gartner went on a rampage at the 1993 All-Star game, scoring four goals to join Wayne Gretzky (1983), Mario Lemieux (1990) and Vincent Damphousse (1991) as the only players to light the lamp four times in an NHL All-Star game. Gartner, who was voted the game's MVP, also set a record for the fastest two goals from the start of an All-Star game by rifling the puck home twice in a 22-second span at 3:15 and 3:37 of the first period, as the Wales Conference drubbed the Campbell Conference 16–6.

6.13 A. Steve Yzerman
Although he had posted five 50-goal seasons and cracked the 100-point barrier six times in his career as of 1996, "Stevie Wonder" has never been elected to either a First or Second NHL All-Star Team. Yzerman has had the misfortune of playing in an era when the centre position was dominated by Wayne Gretzky and Mario Lemieux. Even in years when Lemieux and Gretzky faltered, Yzerman was edged out in the balloting by other talented pivots such as Mark Messier, Adam Oates, Dale Hawerchuk and Pat LaFontaine.

6.14 B. Syl Apps, Jr.
Syl Apps, Sr., the Toronto Maple Leaf great, played in the first NHL All-Star game in 1947. Syl Apps, Jr. followed in his father's skate tracks by appearing in the midseason classic in 1975. The Pittsburgh Penguins centre scored twice in the Wales Conference's 7–1 victory and was voted the game's MVP. Tracy Pratt, son of Hall-of-Famer Babe Pratt, represented the Vancouver

Canucks in the same game, but his father never played in an All-Star game.

6.15 C. Bobby Orr

Eddie Johnston, the former Bruins goalie and current Penguins coach, once said about Orr: "He could thread a needle with a puck, shoot it like a bullet or float it soft. Orr was the only player who could dictate the tempo of the game, speed it up or slow it down. He could see the whole ice the way a spectator sees it from above." A good indicator of Orr's brilliance are the record eight consecutive First Team All-Star berths he earned from 1968 to 1975. If Orr's wonky knees had not prematurely derailed his career, there is no telling how many times he would have been a First Team All-Star.

Consecutive First Team All-Star Berths*

Player	No.	Years
Bobby Orr	8	1968 to 1975
Wayne Gretzky	7	1981 to 1987
Bobby Hull	7	1964 to 1970
Doug Harvey	7	1952 to 1958
Phil Esposito	6	1969 to 1974
Maurice Richard	6	1945 to 1950
Guy Lafleur	6	1975 to 1980

Current to 1996.

GAME 6

THE TOP DEFENSE CORPS

Listed below are the first names of an elite corps of defensemen: all 16 are Norris Trophy winners. Once you figure out their last names, find them in the puzzle by reading across, down or diagonally. As with our 16th example, Bobby O-R-R, connect the names by using letters no more than once. Start with the letters printed in heavy type.

(Solutions are on page 116)

Chris _____	Doug _____	Red _____	Brian _____
Tom _____	Larry _____	Paul _____	Ray _____
Harry _____	Pierre _____	Denis _____	Doug _____
Rod _____	Randy _____	Jacques _____	Bobby _____

```
    R U E   R A C
  L O Q Y L V T O P
  B A R L I N O S Y
  N I P U E N I L A
  S C P E O W A N W
  O H L I R B L C G
  N E O K R S O O H
  L T E L I N N F C
  I E L E H Y E F T
  O Y R O Y E R-R E
  S E W E J R V O E
    H O L L A H L
```

7

READER REBOUND

After the success of Reader Rebound in our sixth hockey trivia book, we decided to publish another chapter of questions from our readers. Again, thanks to everyone for participating. If you didn't make the cut, there is always next year's edition—just fill out the form at the back of the book.

(Answers are on page 72)

7.1 Which two players assisted on the goal that made Wayne Gretzky the highest point scorer in NHL history?

Gilles Michaud
Sudbury, Ontario

7.2 Who holds the record for playing for the most NHL teams?

Dani Berman
Elmont, New York

7.3 Of all the players still active in the NHL in 1995–96, who scored the most points in the WHA?

Ricky Somers
Black River Bridge, New Brunswick

7.4 What colour were the pucks used in the WHA?

Justin Karp
Santa Clara, California

7.5 Who were the three members of the Triple Crown Line?

Shawn White
Lower Sackville, Nova Scotia

7.6 Who scored the first goal in Colorado Avalanche history?

Brent Gaines
Westport, Connecticut

7.7 Who was the first Edmonton Oiler to win the Conn Smythe Trophy as MVP of the playoffs?

Dave Lemley
Coalhurst, Alberta

7.8 Which team has won the most Stanley Cups?

John Webster
Boxboro, Massachusetts

7.9 Which team won the Stanley Cup in the NHL's first season?

Tripp Burnett
Memphis, Tennessee

7.10 How many NHL players have scored 50 goals in 50 games?

Martin LePage
Kincardine, Ontario

7.11 Who scored the overtime goal that put the New Jersey Devils into the playoffs for the first time in the team's history?

Brooke Nowakowski
Sterling Heights, Michigan

7.12 Which NHL player is pictured eating a hot dog in the 1995–96 Pinnacle hockey card set?

James Wallace
Springville, New York

7.13 Who is the all-time leading scorer of NHL players born in France?

Matt Ring
Winnipeg, Manitoba

7.14 In what season did Mark Messier first score 50 goals?

Marc Drouin
Rockland, Ontario

7.15 Which NHL team signed a historic joint-venture sports marketing agreement with Russia's Central Red Army Club in 1993?

Michael Rearick
Apollo, Pennsylvania

7.16 How many NHL goalies have scored a goal?

Michael Fisher
Colonie, New York

7.17 Which NHLer scored the most regular-season overtime goals during the 1980s?

Chris Brown
Moose Jaw, Saskatchewan

7.18 Who was the first player to score a goal in the NHL?

Brian Schuster
Philadelphia, Pennsylvania

READER REBOUND
Answers

7.1 Gordie Howe's career total of 1,850 points was thought to be unassailable, until Wayne Gretzky entered the

NHL and began destroying all existing scoring records. Fittingly, Howe's mark fell in Edmonton on October 15, 1989, the city where Gretzky rose to prominence, during a game between the Oilers and the Kings. Historic point number 1,851 came on a game-tying goal with 53 seconds left in regulation time on a set-up by Gretzky's Los Angeles teammates **Dave Taylor** and **Steve Duchesne**. The game was halted as Howe came out of the crowd to take part in ceremonies honouring the NHL's new point king. Superstitious types insist it was fated to happen when it did. The time of the goal was 18:51.

7.2   **Brent Ashton** owns the record for playing on the most NHL teams. The Saskatoon-born winger suited up for nine different clubs during his 14-year career. Ashton began his odyssey with the Vancouver Canucks in 1979–80. From there, he went to the Colorado Rockies, New Jersey Devils, Minnesota North Stars, Quebec Nordiques, Detroit Red Wings, Winnipeg Jets, Boston Bruins and, finally, the Calgary Flames in 1992–93.

7.3   There were only three former World Hockey Association players still active in the NHL in 1995–96: Mark Messier, Mike Gartner and **Wayne Gretzky**. All played one WHA season, 1978–79. Gretzky was the top scorer of the trio, notching 110 points in a season split between the Indianapolis Racers and the Edmonton Oilers.

7.4   The pucks used in the NHL are always black, but the WHA experimented with **red-, orange-, yellow-, green-** and **blue-** coloured pucks in its first year of operations in 1972–73. The experiment was a failure. The dyes affected the chemical nature of the pucks, making them more susceptible to cuts and chips and causing them to bounce crazily no matter how cold officials got them before the game.

7.5 The Los Angeles Kings boasted one of the NHL's highest-scoring lines during the late 1970s and early 1980s. The Triple Crown Line featured **Marcel Dionne** at centre, **Charlie Simmer** on left wing and **Dave Taylor** on right wing. The trio enjoyed its best season in 1980–81 when Dionne scored 58 goals, Simmer 56 and Taylor 47, and all three tallied more than 100 points.

7.6 Injuries prevented **Valeri Kamensky** from fulfilling his abundant promise in his first four years in the NHL, but the Russian forward served notice on the opening night of the 1995–96 season that things would be different this time around. Kamensky scored the first goal in Avalanche history in the first period and then notched the game winner at 16:07 of the third stanza as Colorado beat the Detroit Red Wings 3–2. Playing most of the season on a line with Peter Forsberg and Claude Lemieux, Kamensky posted career highs in games played (81), goals (38), assists (47) and points (85).

7.7 The Edmonton Oilers thwarted the New York Islanders' bid to win a fifth consecutive Stanley Cup in 1984, dethroning the NHL champions in five games in the finals. Wayne Gretzky led all playoff marksmen with 35 points, but the Conn Smythe Trophy as the playoff MVP went to **Mark Messier**, whose grit and tenacity sparked the young Oilers to their first Cup.

7.8 As of 1996, **the Montreal Canadiens** have won 24 Stanley Cups, far more than any other NHL team. In fact, the Habs have won more championships than any other team in pro sports.

7.9 The **Toronto Blueshirts** (a.k.a. the Toronto Arenas), led by rookie coach Dick Carrol, won the Stanley Cup in the NHL's inaugural season, in 1917–18. Toronto beat the Montreal Canadiens 10–7 in a two-game, total-goals series to take the NHL title, then met the Vancouver Millionaires, champions of the Pacific Coast Hockey Association, in the best-of-five Cup finals. The Blueshirts prevailed three games to two, capturing the deciding fifth encounter 2–1, thanks to a third-period goal by Corbett Denneny.

7.10 Players who have scored 50 goals in their teams' first 50 games of a season make up one of the most exclusive clubs in hockey. As of 1996, just **five NHL players** dot the 50-in-50 roster: Maurice Richard, Mike Bossy, Wayne Gretzky (three times), Mario Lemieux and Brett Hull. Lemieux and three other players—Jari Kurri, Alexander Mogilny and Cam Neely—have also scored 50 goals in 50 games or less, but not in their teams' first 50 games of the season.

The NHL's Exclusive 50-in-50 Club*

Player	Year	Team	Game	Age
Maurice Richard	1944-45	Mtl	50	23.7
Mike Bossy	1980-81	NYI	50	23.1
Wayne Gretzky	1981-82	Edm	39	20.11
Wayne Gretzky	1983-84	Edm	42	22.11
Wayne Gretzky	1984-85	Edm	49	24.0
Mario Lemieux	1988-89	Pit	46	23.3
Brett Hull	1990-91	StL	49	26.5

Current to 1996.

7.11 The New Jersey Devils, perennial also-rans in the NHL's Patrick Division, met the Chicago Blackhawks in the final game of the 1987–88 season, needing a win to make the playoffs for the first time in the club's history. The game, played at Chicago Stadium, was deadlocked after 60 minutes and went into a five-minute overtime. At 2:21 of overtime, Devils winger **John MacLean** became an instant hero when he fired a rebound past Hawks goalie Darren Pang. The game was a personal triumph for MacLean, who also scored the goal that tied the contest and sent it into overtime.

7.12 **Olaf Kolzig** of the Washington Capitals appears in an unusual pose on his 1995–96 Pinnacle hockey card. The South African-born netminder is pictured preparing to munch into a mustard-topped hot dog.

7.13 France has not produced many NHL players, but one of the country's native sons did enjoy a successful big-league career. **Paul MacLean**, who was born in Grotsequin, France, accumulated 324 goals and 348 assists for 673 points in 11 NHL campaigns. MacLean's best years were spent in Winnipeg, where he had three 40-goal seasons.

7.14 As of 1996, Mark Messier has only reached the 50-goal mark once. He notched 50 goals in **1980–81** and 38 assists for 88 points. It is the only season of his career in which Messier counted more goals than assists.

7.15 In 1993, **the Pittsburgh Penguins** made hockey history by entering into a revolutionary, joint-venture marketing agreement with the Soviet Red Army Club. The deal saw control of the Moscow-based team pass to a three-party consortium comprised of Red Army coach Viktor Tikhonov and general manager Valeri Gushin, and Penguins owner Harold Baldwin. The partnership provided the struggling Red Army team with badly needed working capital and NHL-style marketing. In return, the Pens were able to set up a more extensive scouting system in Russia and gain greater access to the available pool of Russian players.

7.16 **Three goalies** have scored a goal in an NHL game: Billy Smith, Ron Hextall and Chris Osgood. Smith received credit for a goal in 1979 when Rob Ramage of the Colorado Rockies accidentally shot the puck into his own net. Ron Hextall scored twice into an empty net: in

1987 versus Boston and in 1989 against Washington. Osgood did it in 1996, when he fired the puck the length of the ice into the empty cage against Hartford.

7.17 **Mario Lemieux** scored seven overtime goals during regular-season play in the 1980s, the best number accumulated by one player in that decade.

7.18 The NHL's inaugural season, 1917–1918, began on December 19, 1917 with two games, the Toronto Blueshirts versus the Montreal Wanderers and the Montreal Canadiens against the Ottawa Senators. Though it is widely believed that both contests were played in Montreal, the Canadiens-Senators game actually took place at the Ottawa Arena on Laurier Avenue. The game, attended by 6,000 rowdy fans, began promptly at 8:30 p.m. The first goal was scored by the Canadiens' Joe Malone at 6:30 of period one. In the other opening game, at the Montreal Arena, Montreal's Dave Ritchie netted the first goal between the Blueshirts and the Wanderers at 1:00 of the first period. Unfortunately, the Montreal game's start time remains unconfirmed. So credit both the Wanderers' **Dave Ritchie** and **Joe Malone** of the Canadiens as the first goal scorers in NHL history.

GAME 7

THE 500-GOAL CLUB

A record four players joined the exclusive ranks of the 500-goal club in 1995-96, the most in any NHL season to date. Thirty years ago, the idea of four players reaching the 500-goal plateau in one season would have been unthinkable. In fact, the league went almost eight years without a new 500-goal scorer from Gordie Howe's 500th in March 1962 to Bobby Hull's 500th in February 1970.

As of 1996, there were 23 NHLers with 500 career goals. Match those listed below with the highlights provided. To make it interesting, some players will be correct for more than one answer.

(Solutions are on page 116)

Mark Messier	Lanny McDonald	Guy Lafleur
Mario Lemieux	Frank Mahovlich	Gordie Howe
Bobby Hull	Johnny Bucyk	Jean Béliveau
Dale Hawerchuk	Stan Mikita	Wayne Gretzky
Jari Kurri	Steve Yzerman	Maurice Richard

1. _____ Who was the first 500-goal scorer in NHL history?

2. _____ Which player needed the most games to score 500 goals?

3. _____ Who are the only two 500-goal scorers from Europe?

4. _____ Which four players scored their 500th in 1995-96?

5. _____ Which three players took the fewest games to reach the 500-goal mark?

6. _____ Among all teams, the Montreal Canadiens have had the most 500-goal scorers wear their jersey; a record four players. Who are they?

7. _____ Who are the only two players to score their 500th against netminders not wearing masks?

8. _____ Who are the only three players to score their 500th into an empty net?

9. _____ Who is the only member of the 500-goal club without 1,000 points?

10. _____ Which 500-goal scorer has the most career penalty minutes and who has the fewest PIM?

11. _____ Who is the only player to end his career with exactly 500 goals?

8

FAMOUS FIRSTS

For every NHL record, there is a player who first establishes the mark. If you've played Game 7, you know that Rocket Richard was the league's first 500-goal man. But often with each record there are surprising spinoffs, or other firsts that the stat books never get around to recording. For example, who was the first player to collect his 500th goal and 1,000th point in the same season?

In this chapter, we spin off and look at some of the more obscure NHL firsts. To get you started, we'll tell you that Frank Mahovlich was the first player to nail his 500th goal and 1,000th point in the same season, 1972–73.

(Answers are on page 84)

8.1 Who was the first NHL goalie to have his number retired?
A. The Rangers' Ed Giacomin
B. The Flyers' Bernie Parent
C. The Red Wings' Terry Sawchuk
D. The Maple Leafs' Turk Broda

8.2 Who was the first NHL player from outside North America to sign an endorsement contract with a Fortune 500 company?
A. Pavel Bure
B. Jaromir Jagr
C. Sergei Fedorov
D. Teemu Selanne

8.3 What NHL first occurred when Detroit met Calgary on October 27, 1995?
A. Calgary became the first team to use three goalies in a game
B. Paul Coffey became the first defenseman to bag 1,000 assists
C. Detroit became the first team to use a five-man Russian unit
D. Trevor Kidd became the first goalie to register two assists in one game.

8.4 Who was the first player from an NHL expansion team to record a 50-goal season?
A. The Flyers' Rick MacLeish
B. The Kings' Marcel Dionne
C. The Sabres' Rick Martin
D. The Islanders' Mike Bossy

8.5 Who was the first player, other than a goalie, to win the Calder Trophy as the NHL's top rookie and be voted to the First All-Star Team in the same year?
A. Bobby Orr
B. Ray Bourque
C. Mike Bossy
D. Pavel Bure

8.6 Who was the first player to play on a Stanley Cup-winning team *before* he won the Calder Trophy as rookie of the year?
A. Ken Dryden
B. Tony Esposito
C. Gaye Stewart
D. Danny Grant

8.7 Who scored the first goal at the Montreal Canadiens' new arena, the Molson Centre?
A. Saku Koivu
B. Pierre Turgeon
C. Martin Rucinsky
D. Vincent Damphousse

8.8 Vasily Tikhonov, son of longtime Soviet national team coach Viktor Tikhonov, became the first Russian-born head coach of a North American pro hockey team when he assumed the reins of which IHL club in 1995–96?
A. The Orlando Solar Bears
B. The Milwaukee Admirals
C. The Kansas City Blades
D. The Los Angeles Ice Dogs

8.9 Who was the first NHLer to collect 100 assists in a season?
A. Bobby Orr
B. Stan Mikita
C. Marcel Dionne
D. Wayne Gretzky

8.10 Who was the first coach of the Quebec Nordiques?
A. Jacques Demers
B. Michel Bergeron
C. Maurice Filion
D. Rocket Richard

8.11 Who was the first player to score a goal in an NHL game *after* he was inducted into the Hall of Fame?
A. Bobby Hull
B. Gordie Howe
C. Guy Lafleur
D. Milt Schmidt

8.12 Who was the first Swedish player to post a 50-goal season in the NHL?

A. Kent Nilsson

B. Mats Sundin

C. Hakan Loob

D. Tomas Sandstrom

8.13 Which was the first expansion club to defeat the Montreal Canadiens in a playoff series?

A. The Buffalo Sabres

B. The Edmonton Oilers

C. The Quebec Nordiques

D. The Minnesota North Stars

8.14 In what decade did the NHL first require teams to dress two goalies for regular-season games?

A. 1940s

B. 1950s

C. 1960s

D. 1970s

8.15 Who is Fred Saskamoose?

A. The first NHL player to wear a helmet

B. The first NHL player to die in action in World War II

C. The first NHL player to score on a penalty shot

D. The first of Canada's aboriginal players to play in the NHL

8.16 Who was the first player from an expansion team to lead the NHL in scoring?

A. Marcel Dionne

B. Bryan Trottier

C. Bobby Clarke

D. Wayne Gretzky

FAMOUS FIRSTS
Answers

8.1 B. The Flyers' Bernie Parent
It is surprising, considering all the great goalies who have played the game, that no puck stopper would have his number retired until October 11, 1979, the date Bernie Parent's No. 1 was taken out of circulation. Parent secured a place in Philadelphia hockey history by leading the Flyers to Stanley Cups in 1974 and 1975. His brilliance between the pipes in those two post-seasons earned him back-to-back Conn Smythe Trophies as MVP of the playoffs and prompted the appearance of a famous placard at the Spectrum: "Only God Saves More Than Parent."

8.2 C. Sergei Fedorov
In October 1995, the smooth-skating Red Wing superstar inked a three-year endorsement deal with Nike Inc., the American shoe and sportswear colossus, to promote its fledgling roller- and ice-hockey divisions. Fedorov and fellow endorsers, Brian Leetch and Scott Stevens, gave the company its first shot of prime-time hockey exposure when they hit the ice wearing new Nike skates, with the famous "Swoosh" logo, at the 1996 NHL All-Star game in Boston.

8.3 C. Detroit became the first team to use a five-man Russian unit
The Red Wings iced five skaters from the former Soviet Union at 1:45 of the first period when they played Calgary on October 27, 1995. The historic moment came on a sequence when each of the five hopped over the boards on the fly. The players were defensemen Viacheslav Fetisov and Vladimir Konstantinov, centre Igor Larionov and wingers Sergei Fedorov and Vyacheslav Kozlov. The unit didn't score on its first

shift, but it did connect later in the period to fire Detroit into the lead, en route to a 3–0 win. Though a few NHL teams have had as many as five Russians dressed in a game, playing five as a unit is unique. It proved to be a tremendous success for Detroit and its general manager and coach Scotty Bowman. For Bowman, the game's supreme strategist, the plan brought together five players who share more than culture or language, but also a style of hockey developed by the great Soviet Red Army teams. Michael Farber of *Sports Illustrated* observed, "Their sense of hockey's geometry is so markedly different than the linear North American concept. Their game is almost circular. Sometimes they pass to open spaces instead of players. They double back. Larionov can delay and delay and delay some more and then hit a streaking winger, giving Kozlov or Fedorov the puck in position to score goals."

8.4   A. The Flyers' Rick MacLeish
The Philadelphia centre become the first player from an expansion team to crack the 50-goal barrier when he notched his 50th goal and his 100th point in the last game of the 1972–73 season.

The First 50-Goal Men of the 1967 Expansion

Player	Team	Year	G	A	PTS
Rick MacLeish	Phi	72-73	50	50	100
Rick Martin	Buf	73-74	52	34	86
Rick Martin	Buf	74-75	52	43	95
Reggie Leach	Phi	75-76	61	30	91
Pierre Larouche	Pit	75-76	53	58	111
Jean Pronovost	Pit	75-76	52	52	104
Bill Barber	Phi	75-76	50	62	112
Danny Gare	Buf	75-76	50	23	73

8.5 B. Ray Bourque

Although six NHL goalies have won the Calder Trophy as top rookie and been voted to the First All-Star Team in their freshman season, the first skater to do both was Bourque, Boston's first pick (eighth overall) in the 1979 entry draft. Exhibiting a poise beyond his years, the 19-year-old Boston freshman scored 65 points in 1979–80, 24 points more than Bobby Orr recorded in his rookie year. Bourque made the First All-Star Team in 1980, ahead of such talented veterans as Denis Potvin, Borje Salming and Serge Savard.

8.6 C. Gaye Stewart

Ken Dryden, Danny Grant and Tony Esposito all played on Stanley Cup winners before copping rookie-of-the-year honours, but to find the first player to turn the trick you have to go back to the 1942 Cup finals between Toronto and Detroit. Trailing three games to none, the Leafs staged a miraculous rally to beat the Red Wings in seven games. Gaye Stewart, a rookie winger called up from the minors for game five, stayed in the Leafs' lineup for games six and seven, thereby getting his name engraved on the Cup after playing only three NHL games. The next season, Stewart was voted the NHL's top rookie to complete the rare double.

8.7 D. Vincent Damphousse

Damphousse scored the first goal at the Molson Centre at 6:13 of the first period in the Habs' 4–2 opening-night win over the New York Rangers. Naturally, the evening featured plenty of firsts. Valeri Bure and Martin Rucinsky recorded the first assists at the new arena, Glenn Healy gave up the first goal, Bill Berg counted the first goal for a visiting team, and Lyle Odelein took the first stupid penalty—for attempting to head-butt the Rangers' Darren Langdon.

8.8 C. The Kansas City Blades
Tikhonov became the first Russian coach in the history of North American pro hockey when he assumed command of the IHL's Blades in October 1995. The position opened up when Kansas City's coach Jim Wiley replaced Kevin Constantine as bench boss of the Blades' parent club, the San Jose Sharks. Tikhonov has a bachelor's degree in teaching and coaching, a masters in biomechanics and is fluent in Russian, Latvian, Finnish and English. Under Tikhonov, Kansas City finished third in the IHL's Midwest Division and was defeated in the first round of the playoffs by the Utah Grizzlies.

8.9 A. Bobby Orr
Boston's fabled No. 4 bagged 102 assists in 1970–71 to become the first NHLer to reach the century mark. In doing so, Orr broke his own record for assists (87), set the previous year. The bowlegged kid from Parry Sound completely revolutionized the role of the defenseman with his slick playmaking and electrifying end-to-end dashes. Before Orr came along, Pat Stapleton held the NHL record for assists by a D-man with 50. The only other players to break 100 assists in a season are Wayne Gretzky (11 times) and Mario Lemieux (once). Orr's 102-assist mark was snapped by Gretzky in 1980–81, when the Great One notched 109 helpers.

8.10 D. Rocket Richard
Richard's coaching career was a brief one. He lasted just two games as the bench boss of the WHA's Quebec Nordiques in 1972–73 before deciding he was not cut out for the job. The Rocket left with a record of one win and one loss and was replaced by Maurice Filion.

8.11 B. Gordie Howe
Howe first retired from the NHL after a 25-year career with the Detroit Red Wings in 1971. The NHL waved its customary four-year waiting period and elected Howe

to the Hall of Fame in 1972. In 1973, Howe made a historic return to hockey, joining the Houston Aeros of the WHA in order to play with his sons, Mark and Marty. Howe spent four years in Houston and two more with the New England Whalers. When the WHA and NHL merged in 1979, he became an NHL Hartford Whaler. On October 13, 1979, the 51-year-old Howe beat Pittsburgh's Greg Millen at 10:23 of period one to become the first player to score an NHL goal after being elected to the Hall of Fame. Guy Lafleur, elected to the Hall in 1988, became the second player to achieve the feat, when he returned to the NHL as a New York Ranger in 1988–89 after a three-year retirement.

8.12 C. Hakan Loob
As of 1996, Loob is the only Swede to register a 50-goal NHL season. The speedy winger hit 50 on the final game of the 1987–88 season with the Calgary Flames. After winning the Stanley Cup with the Flames in 1989, Loob left the NHL and returned home to play with Farjestad in the Swedish Hockey League. In 1995–96, Loob overtook Lars-Gunnar Petterson to become the all-time leading scorer in the Swedish Hockey League.

8.13 A. The Buffalo Sabres
The Buffalo Sabres reached the 1975 Cup finals by defeating the Montreal Canadiens in six games in the Wales Conference semifinals. It marked the first time Montreal had lost a playoff series to an expansion club in seven previous meetings. Ironically, the Sabres, who were led by the high-scoring French Connection Line of Gilbert Perreault, Rick Martin and Rene Robert, employed the same fast-skating, pinpoint-passing style of hockey popularized by the Canadiens.

8.14 C. 1960s
In 1965–66, Toronto Maple Leafs coach and general manager Punch Imlach had his veteran tandem of

Terry Sawchuk and Johnny Bower share goaltending duties. Sawchuk played 36 games and Bower 34. The duo allowed the fewest goals in the league. But when the NHL tried to award the Vezina Trophy to Sawchuk because he had played two more games, he refused to accept it. Sawchuk wanted Bower's name on the trophy too and the prize money split between them. The league relented, and not only changed the rules to allow the award to be shared by the netminders on the team with the lowest goals-against average, but also made it mandatory the next year for teams to dress two goalies for regular-season games.

8.15 D. The first of Canada's aboriginal players to play in the NHL
Saskamoose, a Cree from the Sandy Lake Reserve, Saskatchewan, played 11 games with the Chicago Blackhawks in 1953–54. He recorded no points and six penalty minutes in his brief NHL stint. In 1962, when Saskamoose was a playing coach with the Kamloops Chiefs, the Shuswap and Chilcotin Indians of the B.C. Interior proclaimed him "Chief Thunder Stick," an honourary title he later used when he served as chief of the Sandy Lake Crees.

8.16 B. Bryan Trottier
The New York Islanders lucked out by selecting Bryan Trottier 22nd overall in the 1974 amateur draft. He proved to be the best player in the entire draft. A key member of the Islanders' four Cup-winning teams in the early 1980s, Trottier became the first player from a post–1967 expansion team to top the NHL in scoring when he collected 134 points in 1978–79.

GAME 8

THE HOCKEY CROSSWORD

(Solutions are on page 117)

Across

1. _____ of Alberta
6. _____-season play
8. With 7 down, series of away games
9. The best players
10. Imlach's favourite number
11. Home of the Kings
13. An _____ net
15. Habs' initials
17. Coach gives him the _____ to get out on the ice
20. _____ Mikita
21. 1960 and 70s Leaf-Bruin-Canuck. Mike _____
22. Let it _____
23. San Jose's Todd _____
25. _____ Moog
27. Extra play (abbr.)
28. 1930s Red Wing Larry _____
30. Medical _____
31. Kings' Marcel _____
33. Where Tretiak comes from (abbr.)
34. Hockey's Golden _____
35. Old-time Ottawa-Boston player (full name)
37. Camille _____
39. _____ Deck Cards
40. Isles coach Al _____
44. Playing _____ .500 hockey
45. Borje _____
47. 1995 Cup winners
51. 37 Across's nickname
53. Jersey
54. Calgary-Tampa Bay coach (full name)
56. 1970s Canuck Gerry _____

Down

1. _____ Bruins
2. To be dealt or _____
3. Home of the Leafs (abbr.)
4. In the cellar is in _____ place
5. _____ van Impe
6. _____ a muscle
7. See 8 Across
12. Keith _____
14. He knows his place on the ice at all times (two words)
16. Illegal goal, using your _____
18. _____ Hawerchuk
19. Reed _____
20. Famous Nordiques Czech brothers
22. _____ Gilbert
23. 1960s Bruin Ted _____
24. Messier's uniform number
26. Penguin backup goalie Wendell _____
28. Home of the Ducks
29. 1970-80s Wing-Blue-Oiler Garry _____
30. Even score
32. Home of the Rangers (abbr.)
35. 1980s Sabre-Ranger-Whaler Paul _____
36. Defenseman trophy
38. New York player
41. Awful or _____ pass
42. Goalie Curtis _____
43. The legendary _____ Patrick
46. Pain in the _____
48. Phil's Esposito's nickname
49. Forward position (abbr.)
50. Soviet Red _____ Team
52. Keep the _____ on
55. Forward position (abbr.)

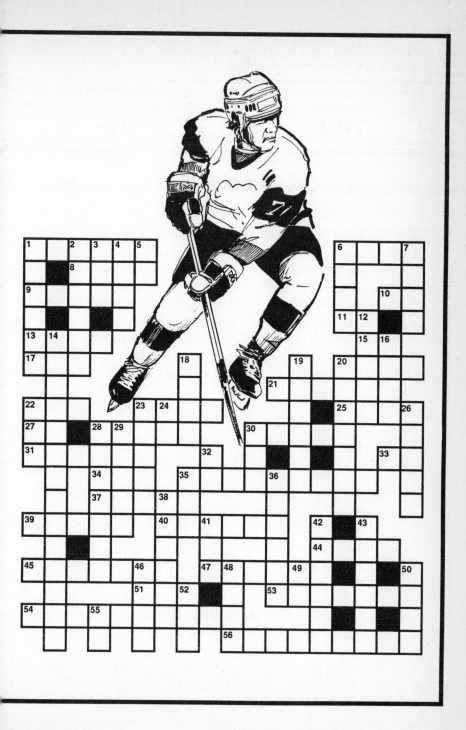

9

TRUE OR FALSE TIP-INS

The Toronto Maple Leafs were the last Original Six team to have a 100-point scorer. *True or false?* It was not until after all five of the other Original Six teams, and three expansion clubs to boot, had produced 100-point scorers that a Leaf finally joined the century club. The player was Darryl Sittler, who hit 100 points right on the nose in 1975–76. Sittler did it once more, notching 117 points in 1977–78. If not for Sittler, Toronto fans would have had a long wait. The next Leaf to reach 100 points was Doug Gilmour in 1992–93.

Before skating into the Stanley Cup chapter, we'll slap a few true- or-false shots at the net and hope for a tip-in. How well you do may depend on how closely you've been paying attention in previous chapters.

(Answers are on page 94)

9.1 **Wayne Gretzky led Edmonton in goal scoring every year he was with the Oilers.** *True or False?*

9.2 **Bobby Orr is the only defenseman to be voted the NHL's most valuable player three times.** *True or False?*

9.3 **A shot on goal is counted when the puck hits the post.** *True or False?*

9.4 **It is illegal to include bonuses for fighting in NHL player contracts.** *True or False?*

9.5 **The first two NHL goals that Tony Esposito allowed were scored by his brother, Phil.** *True or False?*

9.6 Bobby Hull once played for the New York Rangers. *True or False?*

9.7 No player has ever won the NHL scoring title while averaging less than a point per game. *True or False?*

9.8 Guy Lafleur was the first Montreal Canadiens player to score 60 goals. *True or False?*

9.9 No Stanley Cup champion has ever had a Russian-born captain. *True or False?*

9.10 The first Hart Trophy won in 1924 and the first Lady Byng Trophy won in 1925 were both awarded to the same player. *True or False?*

9.11 Steve Yzerman has never been elected to either a First or Second NHL All-Star Team. *True or False?*

9.12 Ray Bourque has been voted to more First All-Star Teams than any other defenseman in NHL history. *True or False?*

9.13 The Mighty Ducks' mascot is called Dizzy. *True or False?*

9.14 Terry Sawchuk was the first NHL netminder to have his number retired. *True or False?*

9.15 Only once since the formation of the NHL in 1917 has there been a year in which there was not a Canadian team involved in the Stanley Cup playoffs. *True or False?*

9.16 Dave "Tiger" Williams was the last NHLer to log more than 400 penalty minutes in a season. *True or False?*

9.17 Henri Richard tallied more career points than his brother, Maurice. *True or False?*

9.18 Mickey Redmond was the Detroit Red Wings' first 50-goal scorer. *True or False?*

9.19 All NHL rink boards are the same height. *True or False?*

9.20 No defenseman has ever won the Lady Byng Trophy as the NHL's most gentlemanly player. *True or False?*

9.21 Jacques Plante ended his goaltending career with the Edmonton Oilers. *True or False?*

9.22 Mike Bossy holds the NHL record for most points in a season by a right-winger. *True or False?*

9.23 A player once scored a hat trick in overtime. *True or False?*

9.24 The distance between Quebec City and Denver is 1,996 miles. *True or False?*

TRUE OR FALSE TIP-INS
Answers

9.1 **False**
Gretzky was topped twice by his Oiler teammates in the club's goal-scoring derby. Jari Kurri (68) and Glenn Anderson (54) scored more goals than Gretzky (52) in 1985–86. Craig Simpson (56) and Jari Kurri

(43) both outscored Gretzky (40) in 1987–88, his last Oiler season.

9.2 False
Boston Bruin defenseman Eddie Shore won four Hart Trophies as MVP, one more than Orr. Shore took the award in 1933, 1935, 1936 and 1938, while Orr won his MVP awards consecutively in 1970, 1971 and 1972.

9.3 False
A shot that hits the post is not considered a shot on goal as it has no chance of going directly into the net.

9.4 True
The Toronto Maple Leafs put blatant incentives for fighting in tough guy Ken Baumgartner's contract in 1995–96—$10,000 for 170 penalty minutes and $55,000 for 260 minutes. But both bonuses were rejected by NHL arbitrator George Nicolau. Other teams circumvent the rule by clever wording. For example, the Hartford Whalers agreed to pay Kelly Chase a $25,000 bonus if he led the league in any statistical category. Of course, the only statistical categories in which Chase would ever lead the NHL are box time or fighting majors.

9.5 True
Goalie Tony Esposito played his first NHL game with the Montreal Canadiens on December 5, 1968, against the Boston Bruins. Big brother Phil welcomed Tony into the big leagues by firing a pair of goals past him in a 2–2 tie. Phil's first goal on Tony came just eight minutes into the game.

9.6 True
Hull joined the New York Rangers for a European exhibition tour in the spring of 1959. The Golden Jet played on a line with the inimitable Eddie Shack. Hull said he changed his style of play on the trip, allowing

Shack to carry the puck instead of trying to do it all himself. The strategy paid dividends as Hull collected 15 goals in 21 games. It also helped him the next year when he scored 81 points and won his first NHL scoring crown.

9.7 False
Four players have won the NHL scoring title while averaging less than a point per game: Bill Cook, Ace Bailey, Sweeney Schriner (twice) and Toe Blake.

Less-Than-a-Point-Per-Game Scoring Champs

Player	Year	Team	GP	G	A	P
Bill Cook	1926-27	NYR	44	33	4	37
Ace Bailey	1928-29	Tor	44	22	10	32
Sweeney Schriner	1935-36	NYA	48	19	26	45
Sweeney Schriner	1936-37	NYA	48	21	25	46
Toe Blake	1938-39	Mtl	48	24	23	47

9.8 False
Lafleur's linemate Steve Shutt became the first Montreal player to reach the 60-goal mark in 1976–77. Lafleur, who finished that season with 56 goals, didn't hit 60 until the next season.

9.9 False
The first Russian-born captain of a Stanley Cup winner was Johnny Gottselig of the 1937–38 NHL champion Chicago Blackhawks. Gottselig, who was born in Odessa, Russia, ended his 16-year NHL career with 372 points in 589 regular-season games.

9.10 True
Frank Nighbor of the Ottawa Senators claimed the Hart Trophy as the NHL's MVP in the award's first year of existence in 1924. He also won the first Lady Byng Trophy as the NHL's most gentlemanly player in 1925.

9.11 True

Yzerman has played in several NHL All-Star games but he has never been elected to either of the NHL's First or Second All-Star Teams, which are chosen at the season's end by the Professional Hockey Writers Association.

9.12 True

As of 1996, Bourque had earned a spot on the NHL's First All-Star Team 12 times, the most of any D-man in league annals. Including his five Second All-Star Team selections, Bourque is a perfect 17-for–17 during his stellar career.

9.13 False

Anaheim's costumed mascot is known as White Wing. His image appears on the Mighty Ducks' new third special occasion jersey.

9.14 False

The distinction of being the first netminder to have his number retired belongs to Bernie Parent, whose No. 1 was retired by the Philadelphia Flyers in October 1979.

9.15 True

In 1969–70, New York and Montreal finished tied for fourth in the NHL's Eastern Division with identical win-loss-tie records, but the Rangers were awarded the final playoff berth because they had scored two goals more than the Canadiens. Montreal's elimination ended a 22-year string of consecutive playoff appearances. Coupled with Toronto's last-place finish, it marked the only time in history that no Canadian team qualified for the playoffs.

9.16 False

Although he is the all-time NHL penalty-minute leader, Williams never topped the 400 PIM mark in any season. Only three NHL enforcers own the dubious distinction of collecting 400 minutes of box time: Dave Schultz, in

1974–75 and 1977–78; Paul Baxter, in 1981–82; and Mike Peluso, in 1991–92.

9.17 True
Henri Richard outscored his older brother Maurice by 81 points (in 278 more games). Henri concluded his career with 1,046 regular-season points, while Maurice compiled 965. Henri also recorded more playoff points (129 in 47 more games) than Maurice (who counted 126).

9.18 True
Redmond became the first Red Wing to score 50 goals in a season when he turned on the red light 52 times in 1972–73. Gordie Howe, a more likely candidate for the honour, fell one goal shy, notching a career-high 49 goals 20 years earlier in 1952–53.

9.19 False
Oddly enough, although the NHL requires exact rink dimensions for everything from face-off circles to goalpost widths, and even precise colour codes for painting the ice surface, there is no one height mandated for the rink boards. NHL rules state that the height of the boards should be between 40 and 48 inches, a variance of eight inches.

9.20 False
Two former Detroit Red Wings, Bill Quackenbush in 1949, and Red Kelly in 1951, 1953 and 1954, both won the Lady Byng Trophy as the NHL's most gentlemanly player while playing defense.

9.21 True
Plante played 31 games for the WHA's Edmonton Oilers in 1974–75 and posted a respectable 3.32 GAA. At age 45, he returned to the Oilers' training camp the next year. But just as the season began, Plante learned one

of his children had committed suicide and he decided to quit the game.

9.22 False

Jaromir Jagr owns the mark. The Penguins' explosive right-winger eclipsed Bossy's record total of 147 by racking up 149 points in 1995–96.

9.23 True

Ken Doraty set a record that can never be broken when he scored an overtime hat trick in a game between the Toronto Maple Leafs and Ottawa Senators on January 16, 1934. In those days there were no sudden-death endings. Instead, the NHL tried to decide tie games with an extra 10-minute period. Doraty netted three goals in the overtime stanza and the Leafs won 7–4.

9.24 True

Cue the *Twilight Zone* theme music. After 16 seasons without even a sniff of a championship, the Quebec Nordiques move to Denver and are renamed the Colorado Avalanche. The Avalanche promptly win the Cup in 1996. Denver is 1,996 miles from Quebec City.

GAME 9

RECORDS UNBECOMING A TEAM

In 1992-93, the Ottawa Senators established the worst road record in NHL history by losing 40 away games. Of those 40 defeats, 38 came consecutively between October 10, 1992, and April 3, 1993, setting another league record for the longest road losing streak. Excluding neutral site games, the 92-93 Senators won just one road game all year, another NHL record.

But Ottawa isn't the sole titleholder of records unbecoming a team. In fact, many other NHL teams hold undistinguished marks, such as the longest losing streak in a season or the most goals against in a season. In this game, match each team's corresponding number (of wins, losses, goals, etc.) with its league record.

(Solutions are on page 118)

Part 1

Washington Capitals - 8
Quebec Bulldogs - 16
Pittsburgh Penguins - 22
New York Rangers - 45
Washington Capitals - 446

Boston Bruins - 11
San Jose Sharks - 17
Chicago Blackhawks - 33
Chicago Blackhawks - 122

1. _____ Most goals against in one season.

2. _____ Longest losing streak in one season.

3. _____ Fewest goals in one season.

4. _____ Most goals allowed in one game.

5. _____ Most power-play goals against in one season.

6. _____ Fewest wins in one season (minimum 70-game schedule.

7. _____ Longest home losing streak in one season.

8. _____ Fewest assists in one season.

9. _____ Most shorthanded goals against in one season.

Part 2

Philadelphia Quakers - 4   Chicago Blackhawks - 8
New York Rangers - 15   Washington Capitals - 21
Winnipeg Jets - 30   San Jose Sharks - 71
Chicago Blackhawks - 83   Chicago Blackhawks - 133
Buffalo Sabres - 2,713

1. _____ Most losses in one season.

2. _____ Most consecutive goals allowed in one game.

3. _____ Longest winless streak in one season.

4. _____ Most shots allowed in one game.

5. _____ Fewest goals in one season (minimum 70-game schedule).

6. _____ Most penalty minutes in one season.

7. _____ Fewest wins in one season.

8. _____ Most consecutive games shut out.

9. _____ Fewest points in one season (minimum 70-game schedule).

10

THE SECOND SEASON

Since the Stanley Cup was first awarded in 1893, some 950 players have skated for championship teams. Better than half (54 per cent—about 530 players) have won only one Stanley Cup, while the rest (46 per cent—about 420 players) have won multiple championships. But how many players in league history have sipped champagne with three different NHL clubs? Or who holds the multiple-team Cup record? At least one of the answers involves a player from the 1996 Colorado Avalanche. Give up? Details follow in our Stanley Cup chapter, The Second Season.

(Answers are on page 106)

10.1 Who set an NHL record during the 1996 playoffs for the most game-winning goals in one playoff year?
A. Joe Sakic
B. Jaromir Jagr
C. Dave Lowry
D. Mario Lemieux

10.2 Rookie coach Doug MacLean of the Florida Panthers almost won the Stanley Cup in 1996. Who was the last coach to sip champagne from Lord Stanley's mug in his freshman season?
A. Harry Sinden
B. Jean Perron
C. Terry Crisp
D. John Muckler

10.3 Who did Colorado Avalanche coach Marc Crawford accuse of causing static interference in his coaches' headsets during the 1996 playoffs?
A. A fan at Florida's Miami Arena
B. CBC-TV broadcaster Bob Cole
C. Detroit head coach Scotty Bowman
D. Chicago general manager Bob Pulford

10.4 On April 24, 1996, the Pittsburgh Penguins and the Washington Capitals played an overtime game that lasted 139 minutes 15 seconds. Where does it rank among the longest games in NHL history?
A. Second
B. Third
C. Fourth
D. Fifth

10.5 Which team beat the New Jersey Devils on the last weekend of the 1995–96 season to eliminate the defending Cup champions from playoff contention?
A. The Boston Bruins
B. The New York Islanders
C. The Ottawa Senators
D. The Tampa Bay Lightning

10.6 Which of these NHL playoff scoring records lasted the longest before it was equalled or broken?
A. Most goals by a player in a final series
B. Most overtime goals by a player in one series
C. Most power play goals by a player in one series
D. Most assists by a defenseman in one series

10.7 Who holds the NHL mark for the most points in a single playoff series?
A. Jean Béliveau
B. Rick Middleton
C. Brian Leetch
D. Mario Lemieux

10.8 Who suffered a life-threatening head injury during a playoff game on March 28, 1950?
A. Red Kelly
B. Gordie Howe
C. Max Bentley
D. Rocket Richard

10.9 During the 1967 Toronto-Chicago semifinals, Bobby Hull fired an errant slap shot over the glass at Maple Leaf Gardens, breaking the nose of a spectator. Who was the unlucky victim?
A. Player agent Alan Eagleson
B. Maple Leafs owner Harold Ballard
C. NHL president Clarence Campbell
D. Canadian prime minister Pierre Trudeau

10.10 As of 1996, Patrick Roy had appeared in 41 playoff overtime games. What is his win-loss record in those games?
A. 24–17
B. 29–12
C. 34–7
D. 39–2

10.11 Which 1996 playoff performer was Colorado Avalanche coach Marc Crawford referring to when he said: "It's almost like he's invisible on the ice. They're looking for him, they know he's around, but they can't find him."
A. Valeri Kamensky
B. Joe Sakic
C. Steve Yzerman
D. Igor Larionov

10.12 During a game in the 1975 Cup finals between
Philadelphia and Buffalo, Jim Lorentz of the Sabres
used his stick to kill a creature that had invaded the
Buffalo Auditorium. What did he kill?
A. A rat
B. A pigeon
C. A bat
D. A snake

10.13 Until Sergei Fedorov surpassed him during the
1995 playoffs, who held the Detroit Red Wings'
team record for most points in one playoff year?
A. Adam Oates
B. Gordie Howe
C. Norm Ullman
D. Bob Probert

10.14 How many players have won the Stanley Cup on at
least three different teams?
A. Four
B. Seven
C. 10
D. 13

10.15 Four different New York Islanders won the Conn
Smythe Trophy as playoff MVP from 1980 to 1983.
Which of these Islanders didn't win the award?
A. Denis Potvin
B. Bryan Trottier
C. Butch Goring
D. Billy Smith

10.16 As of 1996, how many times have goalies won the
Conn Smythe Trophy as playoff MVP in the award's
31-year history?
A. Three
B. Five
C. Eight
D. 10

THE SECOND SEASON
Answers

10.1 A. Joe Sakic
During the 1996 playoffs, the Avalanche captain
stuffed a large sock in the mouths of all the critics who
had previously accused him of lacking leadership
qualities. Sakic's inspirational play and clutch goal
scoring led Colorado to the Cup and earned him the
Conn Smythe Trophy as playoff MVP. Sakic topped all
playoff marksmen with 18 goals and 16 assists for 34
points. His offensive barrage included six game-winning goals, breaking the NHL record of five game winners, shared by Mike Bossy, Tim Kerr, Mario Lemieux
and Bobby Smith.

10.2 B. Jean Perron
In his first season behind the bench of the Montreal
Canadiens in 1985–86, Perron became the 12th NHL
coach to capture the Stanley Cup in his rookie season.
However, Perron was not the only rookie on this
Cinderella squad. The roster included nine freshmen,
many of them promoted from Montreal's farm club in
Sherbrooke, which had won the AHL's Calder Cup in
1985. Ironically, two of the newcomers who were major

contributors to Montreal's miraculous 1986 playoff run—goalie Patrick Roy and right-winger Claude Lemieux—were also key forces on Colorado's 1996 championship team.

10.3 C. Detroit head coach Scotty Bowman
Crawford and Bowman exchanged several insults during the Western Conference finals, but the trash talk hit a new low when Crawford tried to score points by making fun of the head injury that ended Bowman's playing career at age 18. "He's such a great thinker," Crawford said of Bowman. "But he thinks so much that you even get the plate in his head causing interference in our headsets during the game." For the record, a metal plate was not inserted in Bowman's head as part of his medical treatment.

10.4 B. Third
When Petr Nedved beat goalie Olaf Kolzig with 44 seconds left in the fourth overtime period of game four of the Penguins-Capitals Eastern Division quarterfinals, he brought the curtain down on the third-longest game in NHL history. The only two games that lasted longer were played in 1933 and 1936. Both of those contests went to six overtimes. Nedved's game winner hit the back of the net at 2:15 a.m., six hours 37 minutes after the game's 7:38 p.m. start. "It got to the point where I started to think no one would ever score again," said Nedved later. "It's been a long night."

10.5 C. The Ottawa Senators
Few defending Stanley Cup champions have ever plummeted in the ranks as quickly as the 1995–96 New Jersey Devils. The Devils' chances for a playoff berth went up in smoke as they crashed and burned on home ice in their final game of the regular season, losing 5–2 to the last-place Ottawa Senators. The anemic performance prompted coach Jacques Lemaire to declare,

"There has to be a lack of leadership. You can't go out and play a game like that and say this team has leadership." Lemaire should know. He was a member of the 1969 Montreal Canadiens, the last team before New Jersey to suffer the indignity of failing to make the playoffs the year after winning the Stanley Cup.

10.6 A. Most goals by a player in a final series
Cecil "Babe" Dye rattled in nine of the 16 goals the Toronto St. Pats scored in their five-game Cup final series against the Vancouver Millionaires in 1922, establishing an NHL record that has not been equalled or surpassed in 74 years. The other three post-season records were established long after Dye's 1922 mark. The most overtime goals (three) in one playoff series was set by Mel "Sudden Death" Hill in 1939; the mark for most assists (11) by a defenseman in one playoff series was set by Al MacInnis in 1984; and the record for most power play goals (six) in one series was set by Chris Kontos in 1989.

10.7 B. Rick Middleton
An overtime goal by Brad Park lifted the Boston Bruins past the Buffalo Sabres in game seven of the 1983 Adams Division finals, but the real hero of the series was Rick Middleton. The shifty Bruin forward repeatedly bamboozled Buffalo's defense, collecting a single-series record 19 points on five goals and 14 assists.

10.8 B. Gordie Howe
In the second period of game one of the 1950 Leafs-Red Wings semifinals, Gordie Howe stumbled while attempting to lay a body check on Toronto's Ted Kennedy and plunged headfirst into the boards. As Howe lay immobile on the ice, with blood streaming from his forehead and nose, a hush descended over the crowd at the Olympia. The Detroit superstar was taken off the ice on a stretcher and rushed to hospital where he was

found to have suffered a fractured nose and cheek-bone, a lacerated eyeball, a severe concussion and, most serious of all, a brain hemorrhage. Surgeons drilled a tiny hole in Howe's skull to repair the ruptured blood vessel and relieve the pressure on his brain. Throughout the night, radio stations in Detroit and Canada carried updates on his condition. Next morning, the hospital issued a welcome bulletin: Howe was out of danger. He had escaped a skull fracture and there was no permanent damage to his eye. Doctors expected him to recover fully and he did, rebounding to win the NHL scoring title and lead Detroit to the Stanley Cup the following year.

10.9 B. Maple Leafs owner Harold Ballard

The Hawks were engaged in a pre-game shooting drill when Bobby Hull let loose a howitzer that rose over the glass and smashed into Harold Ballard's bunker, 40 feet above the ice. The puck ripped through a program that Ballard was reading, shattering his spectacles and squashing his nose like a ripe tomato. Despite the injury, Ballard didn't hold a grudge. Just before the next game he grabbed a photographer and hailed Hull as the Hawks made their way to the ice. "Bobby, over here!" he hollered, lifting his dented face in profile. "Let's show the world what you've done. Make a helluva photo." It would have, too, but Chicago coach Billy Reay interceded and chased Ballard off.

10.10 C. 34–7

Patrick Roy's reputation as a goalie who thrives under pressure is well-deserved. As of 1996, he had won 83 per cent of the playoff overtime games he had been involved in. During the 1993 post-season, Roy registered an amazing string of 10 consecutive overtime wins for Montreal, including sudden-death victories in games two, three and four of the finals versus the Los Angeles Kings. Time and a change of scenery have not dulled his reflexes. After sudden-death losses to Chicago in games one and three of the 1996 Western Conference semifinals, Roy won four straight games in overtime for Colorado, topped off by a 1–0 double overtime conquest of Florida in the Cup clincher.

10.11 B. Joe Sakic

Like the Romulan space ships in *Star Trek*, Sakic seems to possess his own secret cloaking device. Repeatedly during the playoffs his uncanny offensive instincts enabled him to suddenly materialize on the scene just as a scoring chance presented itself. Crawford's description of Sakic's elusive talents echoes the observation made by Edmonton Oilers general manager Glen Sather, who told a *Hockey News* interviewer in March 1996: "He just sort of drifts in and drifts out. He's almost like the mist. It's there and then it isn't."

10.12 C. A bat

A low-flying bat stole the show during one game of the Sabres-Flyers 1975 Cup finals, until Jim Lorentz abruptly ended the aerial act with his stick. As Lorentz later told a reporter: "The bat was bombing the crowd and people were getting really crazy. Bernie Parent took a few swipes and missed. Then, in the second period, just before a face-off, the bat flew over my head. I hit it on the first swing. Everybody sort of stood around and looked at the thing. Finally, Rick MacLeish took off his glove and carried it in his bare hand to the penalty box." For weeks afterwards, "Batman" Lorentz was inundated with letters. Most who wrote were sympathetic to the plight of the bat, some even called Lorentz "heartless" and "a murderer."

10.13 D. Bob Probert

No, this is not a misprint. Probert tallied 21 points (eight goals and 13 assists) during the 1988 playoffs to set a new Red Wings record for most points in one playoff year. It was an unlikely performance for a player whose offensive contributions are more commonly measured by the number of punches he lands on an opponent's face. Sergei Fedorov finally bumped Probert's name from the top of the team record list in 1995, when he led all playoff scorers with 24 points.

10.14 C. Seven
Seven NHLers have won the Cup on three different championship teams, and prior to 1995–96, the last triple-team Cup winner was Larry Hillman in 1969. Claude Lemieux broke the dry spell, winning championships in Montreal (1986), New Jersey (1995) and Colorado (1996). But no one beats Jack Marshall, the only player to win Cups on four different teams: the Winnipeg Victorias (1901), Montreal AAA (1902), Montreal Wanderers (1907, 1910) and Toronto Blueshirts (1914).

The NHL's Triple-Team Stanley Cup Winners*

Player	Cup-Winning Teams
Jack Marshall	Winnipeg Vics (1901), Montreal AAA (1902/1903), Montreal Wanderers (1907/1910), Toronto (1914)
Frank Foyston	Toronto (1914), Seattle (1917), Victoria (1925)
Harry Holmes	Toronto (1914/1918), Seattle (1917), Victoria(1925)
Jack Walker	Toronto (1914), Seattle (1918), Victoria (1925)
Gord Pettinger	New York (1933), Detroit (1936/1937), Boston(1939)
Larry Hillman	Detroit (1954), Toronto (1964), Montreal (1969)
Claude Lemieux	Montreal (1986), New Jersey (1995), Colorado (1996)

*Current to 1996.

10.15 A. Denis Potvin
Potvin's career was filled with accolades. He won the Norris Trophy as the NHL's top D-man three times, he was voted to the NHL's First All-Star Team five times

and he broke two of Bobby Orr's most cherished career records for a defenseman: most goals and most points. Yet, despite being the captain of all four New York Islander Stanley Cup winners, Potvin never captured the Conn Smythe Trophy as playoff MVP. The Isles' four Conn Smythe recipients were Bryan Trottier in 1980, Butch Goring in 1981, Mike Bossy in 1982 and Billy Smith in 1983.

10.16 D. 10

The spotlight never shines so intently on netminders as it does during the Stanley Cup playoffs. Psychologists estimate that the pressure on a goalie on the day of an NHL playoff game reaches an intensity level most people will only experience once or twice in their lifetimes. A hot netminder can mean the difference between a team winning and losing, which helps explain why these masked marvels have won 10 of the 31 Conn Smythe Trophies awarded to date.

SOLUTIONS TO GAMES

GAME 1: MOST VALUABLE PLAYERS

```
E-U C O-R   Z-T-E-R H
M L R L T R T K H-O-W G U
E F E T A-K-E Y R E L-L X
A S I S O-R O-I F M-I-E-U
L E S P B-E R N E F A-L-P
R M B I O L-I L O-E-G N-T
  I A H E S F V-E-A-U E
I-K T G I R R E L-L-O Y-D
T C-S T A-T A D I-N-S R E
A H O R E A O Y-N-E-R R N
I-M O L C R L O-R D-R I N
D N E-B-A H O S D-N-A C E
  T N-O-C-O   V I-L H K
```

GAME 2: AUCTIONING OFF HISTORY

1. $11,500	2. $900	3. $7,500	4. $15,000
5. $500	6. $2,250	7. $9,750	8. $6,000
9. $1,800	10. $20,000	11. $4,750	12. $3,400
13. $900	14. $2,800	15. $4,000	16. $32,000
17. $12,000	18. $18,500		

GAME 3: TILL THE FAT LADY SINGS

1. "I just give 110 per cent every shift."
2. "He threaded the puck right on the tape."
3. "He signed a multiyear deal for an undisclosed amount."
4. "The game ain't over till the fat lady sings."
5. "Take your game to the next level."
6. "Stay focussed."
7. "Goalies clear the loose rubber and act as a third defenseman."
8. "In the deal, he got fair market value."
9. "He kept his team in the game."

10. "It's a total team effort."
11. "He scored one through the five-hole."
12. "They take the check to make the play."
13. "Enforcers answer the bell."
14. "You can't win if you don't score."
15. "He's a future Hall-of-Famer."
16. "You gotta play through your injuries."
17. "He was slapped with a suspension."
18. "Push your opponents to the brink."
19. "Defense wins championships."
20. "Take it one shift at a time."
21. "There's no tomorrow."
22. "He instigated an altercation and was called on the carpet."

GAME 4: BEHIND THE MASK

The used letters spell out in descending order G-E-R-R-Y C-H-E-E-V-E-R-S, the proud Bruin backstopper who, in the early 1970s, became the first to wear a decorated mask. It was Boston trainer John Forristall who drew black stitches on Cheevers's white mask to indicate where the goalie would have been struck in the face by a puck.

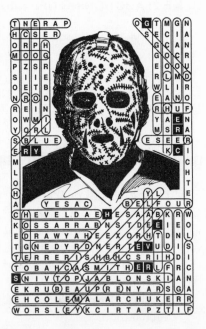

GAME 5: THE EVOLUTION OF AN NHL RECORD

Part 1

1. Joe Malone	44 goals	1917–18
2. Maurice Richard	50 goals	1944–45
3. Bernie Geoffrion	50 goals	1960–61
4. Bobby Hull	50 goals	1961–62
5. Bobby Hull	54 goals	1965–66
6. Bobby Hull	58 goals	1968–69
7. Phil Esposito	76 goals	1970–71
8. Wayne Gretzky	92 goals	1981–82

Part 2

1. Joe Malone	44 points	1917–18
2. Joe Malone	48 points	1919–20
3. Howie Morenz	51 points	1927–28
4. Cooney Weiland	73 points	1929–30
5. Doug Bentley	73 points	1942–43
6. Herb Cain	82 points	1943–44
7. Gordie Howe	86 points	1950–51
8. Gordie Howe	95 points	1952–53
9. Dickie Moore	96 points	1958–59
10. Bobby Hull	97 points	1965–66
11. Stan Mikita	97 points	1966–67
12. Phil Esposito	126 points	1968–69
13. Phil Esposito	152 points	1970–71
14. Wayne Gretzky	212 points	1981–82
15. Wayne Gretzky	215 points	1985–86

GAME 6:
THE TOP DEFENSE CORPS

GAME 7: THE 500-GOAL CLUB

1. Montreal's **Maurice Richard** became the NHL's first 500-goal scorer on October 19, 1957, in his 863rd league game. His victim was Chicago's Glenn Hall.
2. Boston's **Johnny Bucyk** needed 1,370 games to score his 500th, which came on October 30, 1975, against Yves Belanger of the St. Louis Blues.
3. **Stan Mikita** of the former Czechoslovakia and **Jari Kurri** of Finland are the only non-North Americans to reach the 500-goal plateau.
4. In 1995–96, **Mario Lemieux, Mark Messier, Steve Yzerman** and **Dale Hawerchuk** all scored goal number 500.
5. **Wayne Gretzky** (575 games), **Mario Lemieux** (605 games) and **Mike Bossy** (647 games) required the fewest games to score 500 goals.
6. The four 500-goal scorers who have played with the Canadiens are **Maurice Richard, Jean Béliveau, Guy Lafleur** and **Frank Mahovlich.**
7. Neither Glenn Hall nor Gump Worsley were wearing masks when **Maurice Richard** and **Gordie Howe** scored their 500th career goals on them.
8. **Wayne Gretzky, Mike Bossy** and **Jari Kurri** all scored their 500th goals into empty nets.

9. **Maurice Richard** is the only 500-goal scorer with less than 1,000 points. During his 18-year career with the Montreal Canadiens the Rocket scored 544 goals and 421 assists for 965 points.
10. **Gordie Howe** leads all 500-goal scorers in box time with 1,685 penalty minutes. That mark could be passed by Mark Messier, who recorded 1,508 minutes during his 500th goal year, 1995–96. **Mike Bossy**'s 10 seasons netted him just 210 penalty minutes, by far the fewest PIM.
11. **Lanny McDonald** registered exactly 500 career goals from 1973 to 1989. In his final season, he scored 11 times to hit the 500-goal mark.

GAME 8: THE HOCKEY CROSSWORD

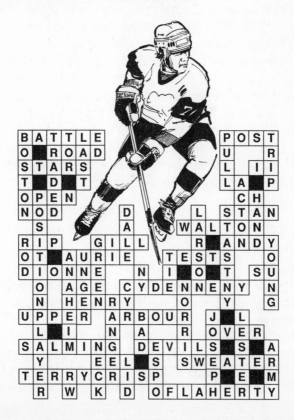

GAME 9: RECORDS UNBECOMING A TEAM

Part 1

1. The **Washington Capitals** hold the NHL record for most goals against (**446**) in one season (1974–75).
2. The **San Jose Sharks** (and Washington Capitals of 1974–75) established the longest losing streak (**17** games) in one season, from January 4, 1993, to February 12, 1993.
3. The **Chicago Blackhawks** scored the fewest goals ever (**33**) in one NHL season, 1928–29's 44-game schedule.
4. The **Quebec Bulldogs** allowed an NHL record **16** goals against in a 16–3 loss to the Montreal Canadiens on March 3, 1920.
5. The **Chicago Blackhawks** allowed an NHL record **122** power play goals against in one season, 1988–89.
6. The **Washington Capitals** recorded only **eight** wins during 1974–75's 80-game schedule, an NHL record.
7. The **Boston Bruins** (and Washington Capitals of 1974–75 and Ottawa Senators of 1992–93) lost **11** home games to set the NHL record for longest home-losing streak in one season, from December 8, 1924, to February 17, 1925.
8. The **New York Rangers** recorded only **45** assists in 1926–27's 44-game schedule, an NHL record.
9. The **Pittsburgh Penguins** of 1984–85 are tied with the 1991–92 Minnesota North Stars for the most shorthanded goals against (**22**) in one NHL season.

Part 2

1. The **San Jose Sharks** lost an NHL record **71** games in 1992–93, one more defeat than the Senators' 70 losses in 1992–93.
2. The **New York Rangers** allowed the most consecutive goals against in one game, losing **15–0** to the Detroit Red Wings on January 23, 1944.
3. The **Winnipeg Jets** suffered the NHL's longest winless streak in one season, **30** games (23 L - 7 T) from October 19, 1980, to December 20, 1980.

4. The **Chicago Blackhawks** established an NHL mark for most shots allowed in one game (**83**), on March 4, 1941, against the Boston Bruins.
5. The **Chicago Blackhawks** scored just **133** goals in 1953–54 to set the NHL record for fewest goals in one season (minimum 70-game schedule).
6. The **Buffalo Sabres** registered an NHL record **2,713** penalty minutes in one season, 1991–92.
7. The **Philadelphia Quakers** (and Quebec Bulldogs of 1918–19) share an NHL record of just **four** wins (in 1930–31's 44-game schedule).
8. The **Chicago Blackhawks** were shut out in **eight** consecutive games in 1928–29, an NHL record.
9. The **Washington Capitals** registered just **21** points in 1974–75's 80-game schedule, an NHL record.

ACKNOWLEDGEMENTS

Care has been taken to trace ownership of copyright material contained in this book. The publishers welcome any information that will enable them to rectify any reference or credit in subsequent editions.

The authors gratefully acknowledge the help of Phil Pritchard and Craig Campbell at the Hockey Hall of Fame, the staff at McLellan-Redpath Library at McGill University, Peter Schaivi and Holly Haimerl of cfcf–12 in Montreal, Robert Clements at Greystone Books, the many hockey writers and broadcasters who have made the game better through their own work, as well as editor Anne Rose, fact checker Allen Bishop, graphic artist Ivor Tiltin and puzzle designer Adrian van Vlaardingen.

HOCKEY TRIVIA'S READER REBOUND

Do you have a favourite hockey trivia question that stumps everyone, or one that needs an answer? Write us, and if we haven't used it before, we may include your question in next year's trivia book. We can only pick about 20 questions and answers, so give us your best shot.

We'll make sure every question selected is credited with the sender's name and city. Just two points: 1) Duplications will be decided by the earliest postmark; and 2) Sorry, we can't answer letters individually.

Write us at: *Hockey Trivia*
c/o Don Weekes
P.O. Box 221
Montreal, Quebec
Canada
H4A 3P5

Please print:
NAME: _____ AGE: _____
ADDRESS: _____
FAVOURITE TEAM: _____
FAVOURITE PLAYER(S): _____
YOUR QUESTION: _____
_____
_____
_____
_____
ANSWER: _____
_____
_____
_____
_____
_____
_____

(continued on next page)

Even if you don't have a trivia question, we'd like to hear from you.

READER SURVEY

In future books on hockey trivia, would you like questions that are:

Easier ❑ About the same ❑ Harder ❑?
Would you like more games ❑; or fewer games ❑?

What kinds of questions or games do you like the most, or would like more of (i.e., multiple choice, true or false, fill-in-the-blanks, crosswords, etc.)?

_____
_____
_____
_____

OTHER COMMENTS: _____
_____
_____
_____

THE OPINION CORNER

What do you like most about hockey? _____
_____

How would you like the game to change (i.e., shootouts, two referees, etc.)? _____
_____
_____
_____

When and how did you first get interested in hockey?_____
_____
_____
_____